The
Common
Names
of
North
American
Butterflies

6-8-99

The

Common

Names

of

North

American

Butterflies

Edited by

Jacqueline Y. Miller

Smithsonian Institution Press
Washington and London

Editor and typesetter: Peter Strupp/Princeton Editorial Associates
Production editor: Eileen D'Araujo
Designer: Susan Cook

Library of Congress Cataloging-in-Publication Data
The Common names of North American butterflies / edited by Jacqueline Y. Miller.
    p.   cm.
   Includes bibliographical references and index.
   ISBN 1-56098-122-9 (pbk.)
   1. Butterflies—United States—Nomenclature (Popular) 2. Butterflies—Canada—
Nomenclature (Popular) 3. Butterflies—United States—Nomenclature 4. Butterflies—Canada—
Nomenclature. I. Miller, Jacqueline Y.
QL548.C66   1992   91-21343
595.78'9097'014—dc20   CIP

British Library Cataloguing-in-Publication Data available

Manufactured in the United States of America

96 95 94 93 92   5 4 3 2 1

Contents

Foreword

When I first became interested in butterflies as a youth in California, I had no book that treated the local species and I had no names, scientific or common, to apply to them. As a result, I invented my own common names. My friends and I developed our own system; for example, the Acmon Blue (*Plebejus acmon*) was the "blue boy," and so on. Of course, if we wanted to communicate about butterflies with anyone else outside our small circle, we were lost. It was not until I began attending meetings of the Lepidopterists' Society and began trying to understand the scientific articles in its journal that I saw a need to learn the scientific names of butterflies. In recent years, as I have served as coordinator for the Xerces Society Fourth of July Butterfly Counts and an advocate of invertebrate conservation, I have seen the desperate need for a standardized list of common names for our butterflies.

The publication of *The Common Names of North American Butterflies*, edited and compiled (in part) by Jacqueline Miller, is a most significant occasion. This is the first serious effort at an "official" standardized common names list for butterflies. It also provides a historical view, since common names used by various past authors are also listed. This is the butterfly equivalent of the American Ornithologists' Union *Checklist of North American Birds*, now in its sixth edition. As such, Dr. Miller's list represents a starting point from which further refinements may be made over the years. I hope that this list will be followed by more finely tuned editions, one hopes not more often than about once each decade.

Although they are not subject to the same nomenclatural rules as the scientific names, it is important that there be some sense of order and stability among the common names. Until now, there has been no stability in the usage of English names for American butterflies. Each current North American butterfly handbook or field guide uses a different array of common names, and this incompatibility makes communication impossible for those who eschew the use of the usually more imposing scientific names. This lack of standardization has meant that some persons who might have taken up an interest in butterflies became discouraged and transferred their affections to a group of animals or plants with names less intransigent to the novice. The growing army of naturalists who wish to learn about butterflies will find their efforts to learn the species much easier with an authoritative common names list. Roger Tory Peterson, the renowned bird artist and author, has stated that butterfly appreciation is now at about the same stage as was birdwatching when his first field guide was published.

Dr. Miller brings to this work considerable expertise in both butterflies and the larger moths. She expended considerable effort in bringing both a sense of urgency and a need for practicality to the selection of recommended names for this list. As such, it was necessary for her to contact and negotiate with persons who campaigned for differing approaches to the selection of common names.

In all likelihood, authors of field guides and other written works on the North American butterflies will now follow the common names used in this listing. For example, the forthcoming field guide to eastern butterflies (Opler, 1992) will use the names listed here. In 1992, the increasingly popular Fourth of July Butterfly Counts sponsored by the Xerces Society will begin to use both the scientific and common names. I imagine that this change will greatly increase the number of counts and will increase the participation of field naturalists and butterfly novices in the counts.

I encourage the readers of this work to apply the recommended names universally, and I hope that authors of all future works on North American butterflies will follow the precedent set by Dr. Miller's extensive efforts.

Paul A. Opler
U.S. Fish and Wildlife Service

Acknowledgments

The compilation of this list has been an extensive project and required the cooperative efforts and contributions of many lepidopterists. The following individuals annotated and provided particular sections: J. Hinchliff and R. M. Pyle (Papilionidae), C. D. Ferris (Pieridae), O. Shields (Lycaenidae, Riodinidae, and Libytheidae), S. S. Borkin and J. Shepard (Heliconiidae, Nymphalidae, Apaturidae, Danaidae, and Ithomiidae), D. M. Lott and L. D. Miller (Satyridae), and J. Y. Miller (Hesperioidea). Paul A. Opler kindly provided the foreword.

The original drafts of each section were submitted to C. D. Ferris, R. O. Kendall, B. A. Mather, P. A. Opler, R. M. Pyle, and J. A. Scott for their critical review and comments, many of which have been incorporated into the text. I am indebted to L. D. Miller and P. A. Opler, who generously provided preliminary lists of common names to be used in their forthcoming publications. Drs. Miller and Opler reviewed the final draft, and their insight into some of the problem areas proved invaluable. I am especially indebted to Carol Kienzlie and Deborah Matthews Lott for their invaluable assistance in the compilation of the index and technical assistance in the production of this list.

Special thanks are due L. P. Brower, P. R. Ehrlich, T. J. Lovejoy, D. D. Murphy, P. A. Opler, R. T. Peterson, and R. M. Pyle for their support and enthusiasm for this project. Their continued dedication to the conservation and preservation of all species and their concern for public education enabled them to recognize the conspicuous necessity for such a list. This project also has benefited immensely from the expertise and extraordinary efforts of Melody Mackey Allen and Mary Troychak, Xerces Society, and Peter Cannell, Smithsonian Institution Press. They and their respective production staffs and consultants are to be commended for bringing this undertaking to completion. To all of the foregoing and to any individuals who may have been inadvertently omitted, my sincere thanks and appreciation for their efforts and cooperation in this most interesting endeavor.

J.Y.M.

Introduction

Have you ever spent a sultry summer afternoon observing clouds of white and yellow butterflies at a mud puddle or walked near a pasture or field road that teamed with butterflies visiting a kaleidoscope of wildflowers? Almost everyone has some fond memories of watching and discovering butterflies. Furthermore, the lives of countless students have been enriched significantly through the study of insect life cycles—in particular the remarkable transition of the caterpillar into the chrysalis and ultimately the adult butterfly.

Beyond the obvious enjoyment and wonder of observing these aesthetically pleasing creatures, butterflies play an important role in the study of our world. Butterflies and their associated larval and nectar host plants are inextricably linked in a process of parallel co-evolution spanning thousands of years. Butterflies use such plants not only for sustenance but also for camouflage and protection. Depending on the specialization of the butterfly, its geographic distribution may also be intimately connected to that of the larval host plant. Thus, butterflies are excellent biological models for the monitoring of different ecosystems and the assessment of conservation practices.

Historically, butterflies, like other organisms, have had two sets of names, the scientific and the common or vernacular names. As man's geographic horizons expanded to include new continents, there was considerable duplication in the use of vernacular names, some of which were applied to completely different entities. The development of binomial nomenclature by Linnaeus (1758) and its subsequent refinement provided stability for the scientific studies. Inevitably, our initial introduction to butterflies has been generally through observations of the Monarch and the Gulf Fritillary, not *Danaus plexippus* or *Agraulis vanillae*.

There have been several scientific treatments of North American butterflies over the years, and recently as many as two or three new regional publications have appeared each year. Traditionally, the early authors, including Scudder (1889, 1893) in particular, adopted both the scientific and the common names. Even today, most novice naturalists do not want to be encumbered by lengthy Latin epithets, which may seem meaningless as far as the actual description of the organism in the field is concerned. In terms of public education, publishers of popular books encourage the use of common as well as scientific names, and federal and other governmental agencies prefer common names for entities designated as potentially threatened or endangered species. Unfortunately, the same common name may have been used to indicate different species, and, as a result, the common name cannot be used alone for the sake of clarity.

HISTORY OF AND RATIONALE FOR THE PROJECT

In 1980, Robert M. Pyle proposed to the Board of Directors of the Xerces Society and to the Executive Council of the Lepidopterists' Society that a joint committee be established to research previously published and proposed common names for North American butterflies, to poll feelings on matters of preference, and to recommend a standardized list of common names. It was felt that such an effort would increase public awareness of butterflies and provide a framework for a popular study of the group. Some twenty knowledgeable individuals from both societies expressed an interest in the project, and Dr. Pyle served initially as Chairman and subsequently as Vice-Chairman. In 1984, the working committee modified the original concept to include a complete list of all common names associated with a particular taxon. Here we have compiled a list of the common names for North American butterflies. This compilation is indicative of the wealth of common names available from one area of the country to the other and denotes the lack of continuity in usage so necessary in a standardized list.

While the rules governing the scientific nomenclature are fixed according to the *Code of Zoological Nomenclature*, usage is the determining factor in the choice of an appropriate common name. Some names, such as the Orange Skipper (*Polites mystic*), Golden Skipper (*Problema byssus*), and Large Brown Skipper (*Calpodes ethlius*), could be applicable to any number of skippers (Hesperiidae), not only in North America but on other continents as well. All of these vernacular names, which were readily associated with the particular taxon in the older literature, have been refined further through the discovery of additional species and through further scientific studies. Other names, such as *Colias meadii* and *Satyrium acadicum*, employ the specific epithet (Mead's Sulphur, Acadian Hairstreak) and are of value in the learning process, while certain common names indicate the larval host plant, such as *Battus philenor*, the Pipevine Swallowtail. Some common names define particular characteristics, such as the distinctive band of the Coral Hairstreak (*Harkenclenus titus*). Thus, many common names do provide some insight into the scientific aspects of butterflies and enable the student to increase his or her proficiency in identification.

The use of butterfly common names has been the subject of great controversy, especially over the past ten years. Most authors, publishers, and state and federal agencies have included common names in their publications to increase their usefulness and to reach a broader sector of the interested scientific public (Klots, 1951; Opler and Krizek, 1984; Pyle, 1984a,b). A wider audience will, it is hoped, engender additional interest in conservation and the preservation of natural habitats for a number of organisms. However, most arguments against the use of common names have involved the coinage of new names that were neither succinct nor totally appropriate (Mather, 1983; Murphy and Ehrlich, 1983; Shapiro, 1975). For example, the Bramble Hairstreak indicates the habitat association of *Callophrys dumetorum,* but the cumbersome Green White-spotted Hairstreak does not. Alternatively, the Bat Blue (*Philotes battoides*), although concise, is not completely descriptive of this delicate, small blue butterfly. And the Banded Orange (*Dryadula phaetusa*) sounds as if it should be a member of the Hesperiidae or the Pieridae, not the Nymphalidae.

There were many heated exchanges in the years 1981–1984 concerning the coinage of new common names; these arguments were set against a background of considerable change in the traditional classification of butterflies and intense discussions of the various analytical approaches (classical, phenetic, phylogenetic) to revisionary studies. Although these deliberations continue, a number of lepidopterists (Ehrlich and Murphy, 1983; Mather, 1983; Miller and Brown, 1981, 1983; Murphy and Ehrlich, 1983, 1984; Pyle, 1984a) still recognize the obvious need for additional biological and systematic efforts. Indeed, the disappearance of once-available habitats for some butterflies and other organisms and the incomplete documentation of the habitat and other biological requirements of a number of butterfly species have added a sense of urgency. Time and fiscal and financial resources are limited for such studies, and many nonetheless feel that our efforts should be directed solely toward scientific ends. Although all of the above viewpoints have merit, we can redouble our efforts by enlisting the aid of other naturalists through effective communication and the usage of common names.

There are at least four significant and compelling reasons for the compilation of a list of common names of North American butterflies. The first of these, as mentioned previously, is that publishers and governmental organizations generally require the common name along with the scientific name and description, to increase the usefulness of a publication. Second, such a readily available compendium of names would prevent the formulation of new names where such coinage is unnecessary. Third, the young and/or novice naturalist may prefer to use the vernacular or common name initially for ease of recognition. At first, scientific names may be confusing or misleading and may pose unnecessary barriers. As their knowledge of butterflies expands, these students generally also begin to increase their proficiency with the scientific names.

Finally, and most noteworthy, is the role that usage of common names plays in the conservation of butterflies through the efforts of such scientific organizations as the Xerces and Lepidopterists' Societies. These societies, often in cooperation with other conservation organizations, have thus far been instrumental in obtaining protection for some individual species under the Endangered Species Act. Public support for such conservation efforts has increased markedly when they are described as directed toward preservation of the Mission Blue or the El Segundo Blue rather than *Icaricia icarioides missionensis* or *Euphilotes battoides allyni*. The usage of common names has been of tremendous educational value in increasing public awareness in such cases. Effective communication through the use of common names has made most naturalists more cognizant that the decline of butterfly populations, particularly of these targeted species, is only one indication of more widespread habitat depletion and the deterioration of natural surroundings. The preservation of the delicate balance of nature depends on the communal relationship that we, as stewards of this planet, must conserve and protect for future generations.

HOW TO USE THIS LIST

This list includes all recorded species and subspecies of North American butterflies distributed north of Mexico and also includes Hawaii. The format for this work is based on the classification and order of L. D. Miller and F. Martin Brown (1981), with modifications by other authors (Bridges, 1989; Ferris, 1989; Opler, 1992). Proper grammatical notation for common names follows that of Parkes (1978) and that which has been traditionally employed. Within the last ten years, the International Commission on Zoological Nomenclature (ICZN) has made significant changes with regard to appropriate usage and gender endings. All modifications in the scientific nomenclature included here, along with the common names, have been or will shortly be published elsewhere. The bibliography includes all of the references consulted for common names as well as references cited in the text. For ease of usage, a complete index to scientific and common names is provided.

The list is presented in columnar format with the scientific name to the left and the associated vernacular or common names on the right. All of the published common names associated with a particular species derived from the references cited are listed, with the preferred name, usually the common name most frequently associated with a particular species, in **boldface.** The subspecies and their vernacular names, sometimes different from those of the nominate species, are also listed. Some authors (Miller, 1991; Opler, 1992; Opler and Krizek, 1984) have generally used the common name most often associated with the nominate species for the subspecies as well, while other authors (Klots, 1951; Pyle, 1974, 1981; Tilden and Smith, 1986) have designated different names for each subspecies. The latter approach has been quite useful in conservation issues. For the sake of space, repetition of the preferred name for the species has been omitted with each subspecific designation except in a few cases for extralimital taxa.

In order to impart some of the historical nuances and better correlate the common names in current usage, the frequency of use for each name has been annotated with the following references which present broader coverage of geographical areas of North America:

H	Holland, W. J. (1931)
Hw	Howe, W. H. (1975)
K	Klots, A. B. (1951)
M	Miller, L. D. (1991)
O	Opler, P. A. (1992)
OK	Opler, P. A., and G. O. Krizek (1984)
P	Pyle, R. M. (1981)
So	Scott, J. A. (1986)
S	Scudder, S. H. (1893)
TS	Tilden, J. W., and A. C. Smith (1986)

AREA OF THIS LIST

Traditionally, the study of butterflies has been limited geographically to a particular state or region. As a convenient general indication of geographical distribution at the species level, the United States has been divided into quadrants west and east of the Mississippi River, and north and south of 40° north latitude.

The key to the geographical regions is as follows:

1	U.S. west of Mississippi River, north of 40° north latitude
2	U.S. west of Mississippi River, south of 40° north latitude
3	U.S. east of Mississippi River, north of 40° north latitude
4	U.S. east of Mississippi River, south of 40° north latitude
A	Alaska
C	Canada
H	Hawaii
W	Widespread

For example, a species such as the Mormon Fritillary (*Speyeria mormonia*) is distributed in the western U.S. (1,2) in addition to Alaska (A) and Canada (C). Blackburn's Blue (*Vaga blackburni*) is limited to Hawaii (H). Some species, such as the Monarch (*Danaus plexippus*), are quite widespread (W).

The reader should consult more specialized references listed in the bibliography for detailed geographical distributions for a particular taxon.

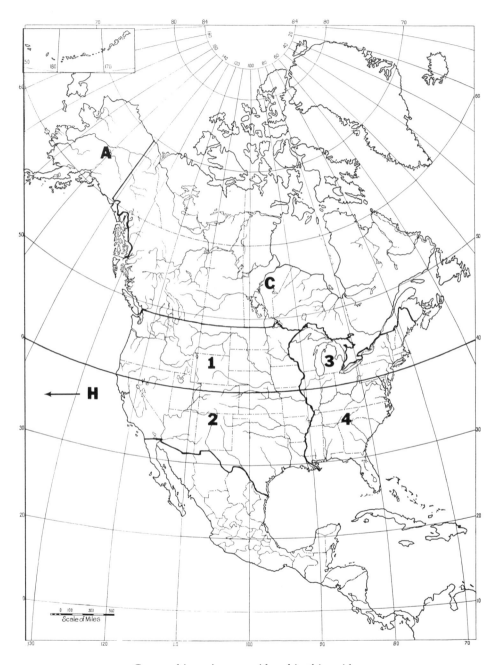

Geographic regions considered in this guide.

OTHER ABBREVIATIONS

* Taxon (usually a species) with a separate subspecies that has a resident population in the geographic area listed.

E Species and/or subspecies accorded endangered status by the Department of Interior, U.S. Fish and Wildlife Service.

T Species and/or subspecies accorded threatened status by the Department of Interior, U.S. Fish and Wildlife Service.

† Extinct

? Species and/or subspecies of questionable occurrence in a particular geographic region.

SPELLING AND VARIATION

Variations in spelling provide some sense of perspective and history. For example, the yellow pierid butterflies are called sulfurs or sulphurs. The term is derived from the Latin word *sulphur* and all other spellings are considered variant. Modern usage does change such spellings, but continuity is the key in any list. With the number of American English dialects and the language variations that occur in other areas of the English-speaking world, such differences are not uncommon.

As you peruse the list, you will note the interchangeable usage of names. While the name fritillary has been associated with a number of genera (*Agraulis, Speyeria, Clossiana*), silverspot has also been used. Agave borer and giant skipper have also been employed with the Megathymidae. This list provides a wealth of information so that an author or student can select the appropriate common name.

The compendium that follows is offered to all enthusiastic lepidopterists, both professional and amateur, in the hope that it will provide a convenient reference. To the latter, we offer an open invitation to further their scientific curiosity through additional biological studies and hope that this work among others will stimulate them to undertake future scientific investigations.

J. Y. Miller, Chairman and Editor
Committee on the Consensus for Common Names
Allyn Museum of Entomology/
Florida Museum of Natural History
Sarasota, Florida

Common Names

Superfamily **HESPERIOIDEA**

Family **HESPERIIDAE—Skippers**

Subfamily **Pyrrhopyginae—Firetail Skippers**

Pyrrhopyge araxes (2)   **Araxes Skipper** P,TS
    Golf Club Skipper So
    Ochery Skipper
    a. arizonae   Arizona Araxes Skipper TS

Subfamily **Pyrginae—Pyrgine Skippers**

Phocides pigmalion (4)   **Mangrove Skipper** K,O,OK,P,So
    p. okeechobee   Batabano Skipper H
Phocides polybius (2)   **Bloody Spot** H
    p.lilea   Guava Skipper O,P,So
    Red-spotted Greenwing

Phocides urania (2)   **Urania Skipper** H,P
    Clear-spotted Greenwing
    Rainbow Skipper So

Proteides mercurius (2,4)   **Mercurial Skipper** O,OK,P
    Idas Skipper H

    m. sanantonio   Mercurial Skipper
Epargyreus zestos (4)   **Zestos Skipper** H,K,OK,P
    Rusty Skipper O,So

Epargyreus clarus (W)   **Silver-spotted Skipper** H,K,M,O,OK,So,TS
    White-spotted Skipper
    Locust Skipper Butterfly
    Silver-spotted Hesperid So

    c. huachuca   Arizona Silver-spotted Skipper TS
    c. californicus   Silver-spotted Skipper
Epargyreus exadeus (2)   **Exadeus Skipper** H,O
    e. cruza

9

Polygonus leo (2,4)	**Hammock Skipper** K,O,OK,P,TS
	Key West Skipper
	Violet Skipper So
l. histrio	Skinner's Arizona Skipper
	Arizona Hammock Skipper TS
	Violet Skipper
Polygonus manueli (2,4?)	**Manuel's Skipper** K,O,P
	Tidal Skipper So
Chioides catillus (2)	**White-striped Longtail** O,P
	Silver-banded Skipper So
	Catillus Longtail TS
c. albofasciatus	White-striped Longtail H,K,TS
	White-banded Skipper
Chioides zilpa (2)	**Zilpa Longtail** H,K,O,P
z. namba	
Aguna asander (2)	**Gold-spot Aguna** O,P
Aguna claxon (2)	**Emerald Green Aguna** O
Aguna metophis (2)	**Tailed Aguna** O
Typhedanus undulatus (2)	**Mottled Longtail** O
Polythrix mexicana (2)	**Mexican Polythrix** O
Polythrix octomaculata (2)	**Eight-spotted Polythrix** O
Polythrix procera (2)	
Zestusa dorus (2)	**Short-tailed Arizona Skipper** H,P,So
	Short-tailed Skipper TS
Codatractus alcaeus (2)	**Alcaeus Skipper** H,O
Codatractus melon (2)	**Melon Skipper** H,P
Codatractus arizonensis (2)	**Arizona Skipper** P,TS,So
Urbanus proteus (2,3,4)	**Long-tailed Skipper** H,K,O,OK,P,So,S, TS
	Common Long-tail Skipper
	Bean Leaf Roller P
	Long-tailed Hesperiid
Urbanus pronus (2)	**Short-tailed Green Longtail** O
Urbanus esmeraldus (2)	**Esmeralda Longtail** O
Urbanus dorantes (2,4)	**Dorantes Skipper** H,K,O,OK,TS
	Lilac-banded Longtail P
	Brown-tailed Skipper So
d. santiago	
Urbanus teleus (2)	**Teleus Longtail** O,P
Urbanus tanna (2)	**Tanna Longtail** O

Urbanus simplicius (2)   **Plain Longtail** O
Simplicius Skipper H,K

Urbanus procne (2)   **Brown Longtail** O,P

Urbanus doryssus (2)   **White-tailed Skipper** O,P,So

* *Astraptes fulgerator* (2)   **Flashing Astraptes** K,O,P
Blue Flasher So

  f. azul

Astraptes alector (2)   **Mad Flasher** So

Astraptes egregius (2)   **Green Flasher** O,So

* *Astraptes alardus* (2)   **White Flasher** O,So
  a. latia

Astraptes gilberti (2)   **Gilbert's Flasher** O

* *Astraptes galesus* (2)
  g. cassius

* *Astraptes anaphus* (2)   **Yellow Flasher** O,So
Dull Astraptes P

  a. annetta

Autochton cellus (2,3,4)   **Golden-banded Skipper** H,K,O,OK,P,
    So,TS
Yellow-banded Brown Wing

Autochton pseudocellus (2)   **False Golden-banded Skipper** P
Arizona Banded Skipper TS
Coolidge's Skipper H
Little Golden-banded Skipper So

Autochton cinctus (2)   **White-banded Skipper** So

Achalarus lyciades (2,3,4)   **Hoary Edge** H,K,O,OK,P,So,S
Frosted Skipper
Hoary Skipper
White-bordered Skipper Butterfly

Achalarus casica (2)   **Desert Hoary Edge** O,So
Mexican Hoary Edge P
Casica Skipper TS
Butler's Dusky Wing H

Achalarus albociliatus (2)   **Skinner's Dusky Wing** H

Achalarus toxeus (2)   **Coyote Skipper** K,O,P

Thessia jalapus (2)   **Jalapus Skipper** O,P

Thorybes bathyllus (1,2,3,4,C)   **Southern Cloudy Wing** K,O,OK,P,S
White-spotted Tailed Brown
Eastern Cloudy Wing So

Thorybes pylades (W)   **Northern Cloudy Wing** H,K,M,O,OK,
                                      P,S,TS
                                  Dark Brown Tailed Skipper
                                  Cloudy Wing So
                                  Suffused Cloudy Wing TS

Thorybes diversus (1,2)   **Western Cloudy Wing**
                                  Bell's Cloudy Wing
                                  California Cloudy Wing So
                                  Diverse Cloudy Wing TS

Thorybes mexicanus (1,2)   **Mexican Cloudy Wing** H,P,TS
                                  Mountain Cloudy Wing So

  m. nevada   Nevada Cloudy Wing TS
                                  Nevada Brown
                                  Aemilea's Cloudy Wing TS

  m. dobra   Dobra Cloudy Wing TS
                                  Mrs. Owen's Dusky Wing H

  m. blanco   Scott's Cloudy Wing TS

Thorybes confusis (2,4)   **Confused Cloudy Wing** K,O,OK
                                  Eastern Cloudy Wing P
                                  Bell's Cloudy Wing H
                                  Dark Cloudy Wing

Thorybes drusius (2)   **Drusius Cloudy Wing** P,TS
                                  White-fringed Cloudy Wing So
                                  Drusius Skipper H
                                  Drusius Brown Wing

Thorybes valerianus (2)   **Valeriana Cloudy Wing** P
                                  Dyar's Skipper H
                                  Mexican Cloudy Wing So

Cabares potrillo (2)   **Potrillo Skipper** K,O,P
                                  Lucas Skipper

Celaenorrhinus fritzgaertneri (2) **Fritz Skipper** O
Celaenorrhinus stallingsi (2)   **Stallings' Skipper** O
Dyscophellus euribates (2)   **Euribates Skipper** H,O
Spathilepia clonius (2)   **Falcate Skipper** O,P,So
                                  Clonius Skipper K

Cogia calchas (2)   **Calchas Skipper** H,K,O
                                  Mimosa Skipper P,So

Cogia hippalus (2)   **Acacia Skipper** O,P
                                  Acacia Brown Wing

	Hippalus Skipper H,TS
	White-edged Skipper So
Cogia outis (2)	**Outis Skipper** H,K,O,OK,TS
	Texas Acacia Skipper So
Cogia caicus (2)	**Caicus Skipper** P,TS
	Arizona White-edged Skipper So
	Schaeffer's Skipper H
c. moschus	Moschus Brown Wing
Cogia mysie (2)	**Mysie Skipper** TS
	Dyar's Skipper H
Arteurotia tractipennis (2)	**Arteurotia Skipper** O
Nisoniades rubescens (2)	**Purplish-black Skipper** O,P,So
Pellicia angra (2)	**Confused Pellicia** O
Pellicia arina (2)	**Glazed Pellicia** O
Pellicia dimidiata (2)	**Morning Glory Pellicia** O
Bolla clytius (2)	**Mottled Bolla** O
Bolla brennus (2)	**Obscure Bolla** O
Staphylus ceos (2)	**Ceos Skipper** H,O,TS
	Golden-headed Sooty Wing P
	Red-head Sooty Wing So
	Ceos Sooty Wing TS
Staphylus mazans (2)	**Southern Scalloped Sooty Wing** O,P
	Mazans Sooty Wing K
	Tropical Sooty Wing So
Staphylus hayhurstii (2,3,4,C)	**Scalloped Sooty Wing** O,P,So
	Hayhurst's Sooty Wing
	Hayhurst's Skipper H
	Southern Sooty Wing TS
Staphylus azteca (2)	**Aztec Sooty Wing** So
*Gorgythion begga (2)	**Variegated Skipper** O,P,So
b. pyralina	
*Sostrata bifasciata (2)	**Blue-studded Skipper** O
b. nordica	
Carrhenes canescens (2)	**Hoary Skipper** O,P,So
Xenophanes trixus (2)	**Glassy-winged Skipper** H,K,O
	Window-winged Skipper P
	Glassy-wing Skipper So
Antigonus emorsus (2)	
Systasea pulverulenta (2)	**Texas Powdered Skipper** O,P

Powdered Skipper So,TS

Systasea zampa (2) **Arizona Powdered Skipper** P,So
Edwards' Powdered Skipper TS
Zampa Gray Wing

*Achlyodes mithridates (2) **Sickle-winged Skipper** H,K,O,OK,P,So
Bat Skipper So
Jung's Dusky Wing
Thraso Skipper

m. tamenund
Grais stigmatica (2) **Hermit** O,P,So
Grais Skipper K
Stigmatic Dusky Wing H

Timochares ruptifasciatus (2) **Brown-banded Skipper** H,O,OK,P,So
Broken-barred Dusky Wing
Timochares Skipper K

*Chiomara asychis (2) **Asychis Skipper** H,K,O,TS
White Patch P
White Patch Skipper So
St. Vincent Grizzled Skipper

a. georgina Asychis Skipper
*Gesta gesta (2) **Common Dusky Wing** TS
Blue-banded Skipper P,S
False Dusky Wing O,So
Gesta Dusky Wing K
Antillean Dusky Wing H

g. invisus Gesta Dusky Wing
*Ephyriades brunneus (4) **Florida Dusky Wing** P
Jamaican Dusky Wing
Caribbean Dusky Wing So
Brown Skipper H

b. floridensis Florida Dusky Wing K,O,OK
Erynnis icelus (W) **Dreamy Dusky Wing** H,K,M,O,OK,P,S,TS
Aspen Dusky Wing So
Small Bluish Skipper
Least Dingy Skipper
Small Bluish-banded Skipper

Erynnis brizo (1,2,3,4,C) **Sleepy Dusky Wing** H,K,M,O,OK,P,
S,TS
Black Skipper

	Banded Oak Dusky Wing So
	Bluish Skipper
	Lesser Dingy Skipper
	Large Bluish-winged Skipper
	Brizo Dusky Wing
b. sommnus	Dark Dusky Wing H
b. burgessi	Burgess's Dusky Wing H,K,TS
b. lacustra	Lacustra Dusky Wing TS
	Wright's Dusky Wing H
Erynnis juvenalis (W)	**Juvenal's Dusky Wing** H,K,M,O,OK,P, S,TS
	Eastern Oak Dusky Wing So
	Juvenal's Skipper
	Seven Spotted-banded Skipper
j. clitus	Clitus Dusky Wing H,TS
Erynnis telemachus (1,2)	**Rocky Mountain Dusky Wing** P
	Gambel Oak Dusky Wing So
	Telemachus Dusky Wing TS
Erynnis propertius (1,2,C)	**Propertius Dusky Wing** H,K,P,TS
	Western Oak Dusky Wing So
Erynnis meridianus (2)	**Meridian Dusky Wing** K,O,TS
	Southern Dusky Wing
	Western Oak Dusky Wing So
Erynnis scudderi (2)	**Scudder's Dusky Wing** H,P,TS
	Arizona Dusky Wing So
Erynnis horatius (W)	**Horace's Dusky Wing** H,K,O,OK,P,S,TS
	Horatius Dusky Wing
	Brown Dusky Wing So
	Florida Brown Skipper
Erynnis tristis (2)	**Mournful Dusky Wing** P,O,TS
	White-edged Dusky Wing So
	Tristis Dusky Wing Skipper
	Sad Dusky Wing H
t. tatius	Tatius Dusky Wing H,TS
Erynnis martialis (W)	**Mottled Dusky Wing** K,M,O,OK,P,So, TS
	Martial's Dusky Wing H,S
	Dark Banded Skipper
	Diminutive Dusky Wing S

Erynnis pacuvius (1,2,C)   **Pacuvius Dusky Wing** H,M,P,TS
                                    Blackthorn Dusky Wing
                                    Buckthorn Dusky Wing So
  p. lilius   Dyar's Dusky Wing TS
  p. perniger   Grinnell's Dusky Wing TS
  p. callidus   Artful Dusky Wing H,TS
Erynnis zarucco (2,3,4)   **Zarucco Dusky Wing** K,O,OK,P,So
                                    Streamlined Dusky Wing So
                                    Lucas' Dusky Wing
                                    Terence's Dusky Wing H,S
Prynnis funeralis (1,2,3,4)   Funereal Dusky Wing H,K,O,OK,P,TS
                                    Mourning Brown
                                    Streamlined Dusky Brown So
Erynnis lucilius (1,3,4,C)   **Columbine Dusky Wing** O,OK,P,So,S
                                    Lucilius Dusky Wing H
                                    Five-spotted Skipper
Erynnis baptisiae (1,2,3,4,C)   **Wild Indigo Dusky Wing** K,M,O,OK,P
                                    Indigo Dusky Wing So
                                    Baptisia Dusky Wing
Erynnis afranius (1,2,C)   **Afranius Dusky Wing** H,P,TS
                                    Bald Dusky Wing So
                                    Dark Skipper
Erynnis persius (1,2,3,A,C)   **Persius Dusky Wing** H,K,M,O,OK,P,S,
                                      TS
                                    Six-spotted Skipper
                                    Hairy Dusky Wing So
                                    Six-spotted Banded Skipper
  p. borealis   Boreal Dusky Wing TS
  p. avinoffi   Avinoff's Dusky Wing H
  p. fredericki   Frederick's Dusky Wing TS
                                    Freeman's Dusky Wing
* *Pyrgus centaureae* (W)   **Grizzled Skipper** H,K,M,O,So,TS
                                    Grizzled Checkered Skipper
                                    Grizzled Tessellated Skipper
                                    Alpine Checkered Skipper P
                                    Grizzled Tessellate S
  c. freija   Freija's Grizzled Skipper TS
  c. wyandot   Wyandot
                                    Grizzled Skipper OK

	Southern Grizzled Skipper
c. loki	Loki Grizzled Skipper TS
Pyrgus ruralis(1,2,C)	**Two-banded Checkered Skipper** M,P,So, TS
	Two-banded Skipper H
r. lagunae	
Pyrgus xanthus (2)	**Southern Checkered Skipper** P
	Xanthus Skipper H,TS
	Xanthus Checkered Skipper
	Mountain Checkered Skipper So
	Checkerling
Pyrgus scriptura (1,2,C)	**Small Checkered Skipper** H,M,P,So,TS
	Small Checker Skipper
Pyrgus communis (W)	**Checkered Skipper** K,M,O,OK,So,TS
	Common Checkered Skipper P,TS
	Common Checker-spot H
	Checkered Hesperiid
	Variegated Tessellate
	Black and White Skipper
	Georgia Grizzled Skipper
Pyrgus albescens (2)	**Western Checkered Skipper**
	White Checkered Skipper P
	Southern Checkered Skipper TS
Pyrgus oileus (2,4)	**Tropical Checkered Skipper** K,O,OK,P, So
	Blue-gray Skipper H
	Syrictus
	Reakirt's Skipper H
Pyrgus philetas (2)	**Philetas Skipper** H,K,O,TS
	Desert Checkered Skipper P,So
	Texas Checkered Skipper
Heliopetes domicella (2)	**Erichson's Skipper** H,K,O,TS
	White-banded Skipper P
	Banded White Skipper So
Heliopetes ericetorum (1,2)	**Large White Skipper** H,P,TS
	Great Basin White Skipper So
	Great White Skipper
	White Checker
Heliopetes lavianus (2)	**Laviana Skipper** H,K,O,P,TS

	Tropical White Skipper So
	Oceanus Skipper
Heliopetes macaira (2)	**Macaira Skipper** H,K,O,TS
	Brown-margined White Skipper So
	Brown and White Checker
Heliopetes arsalte (2)	**Common White Skipper**
	Arsalte Skipper P
	Black-veined White Skipper O,So
Celotes nessus (2)	**Streaky Skipper** K,O,OK,So,TS
	Common Streaky Skipper P
	Nessus Skipper H
Celotes limpia (2)	**Scarce Streaky Skipper** P
	Chisos Streaky Skipper So
	Burn's Skipper TS
Pholisora catullus (W)	**Common Sooty Wing** K,M,O,OK,P,So, TS
	Pigweed Skipper
	Sooty Wing H,S
	Sooty Skipper
	Black Skipper Butterfly
	White-dotted Black Skipper
	Roadside Rambler So
Pholisora mejicana (2)	**Mexican Sooty Wing** H,O,P,TS
	Blue Sooty Wing So
Hesperopsis libya (1,2,C)	**Mohave Sooty Wing** H,TS
	Great Basin Sooty Wing P,So
	Libya Black-wing
l. lena	Lena's Black
	Lena's Sooty Wing
	Lena Sooty Wing TS
	Montana Sooty Wing H,M
Hesperopsis alpheus (1,2)	**Saltbush Sooty Wing** O,P,So
	Alpheus Sooty Wing H,TS
	New Mexican Sooty Wing
a. oricus	Oricus Sooty Wing
a. texanus	Texas Sooty Wing
Hesperopsis gracielae (2)	**MacNeill's Sooty Wing** P,TS
	Saltbush Sooty Wing So

Subfamily **Heteropterinae**

*Carterocephalus palaemon (W)	**Arctic Skipper** H,K,O,P
	Arctic Skipperling So
p. mandan	Arctic Skipper H,M,OK,S,TS
	Dwarf Skipper
	Small Black-checkered Skipper
Piruna pirus (1,2)	**Pirus Skipperling** H,P,TS
	Russet Skipperling P,So
Piruna polingii (2)	**Spotted Skipperling** P,So
	Poling's Skipperling H,TS
Piruna microstictus (2)	**Small-spotted Skipperling** H,O,TS
	Tamaulipas Skipperling So
	Mexican Skipperling
Piruna haferniki (2)	**Hafernik's Skipperling** TS
	Chisos Skipperling So

Subfamily **Hesperiinae—Hesperiine Skippers**

*Synapte malitiosa (2)	**Malicious Shady Skipper** K,O
	Malicious Skipper P
	Shady Skipper So
	The Drab
m. pecta	
Synapte salenus (2)	**Salenus Skipper** O,P
Synapte syraces (2)	
Corticea corticea (2)	**Redundant Swarthy Skipper** O,So
Callimormus saturnus (2)	
Vidius perigenes (2)	**Perigenes Skipper** O
Monca tyrtaeus (2)	**Violet Patch Skipper** O,P
	Tyrtaea Skipper K
Nastra lherminier (2,3,4)	**Swarthy Skipper** K,O,OK,P,So
	Fuscous Skipper H
	Blackish Skipper
Nastra julia (2)	**Julia's Skipper** K,O,TS
	Julia Skipper P
	Western Swarthy Skipper So
Nastra neamathla (2,4)	**Neamathla Skipper** H,K,O,OK,P,TS
	Southern Swarthy Skipper So
Cymaenes tripunctus (4)	**Three-spotted Skipper** K,P

Dingy Dotted Skipper So
Three-spot Skipper O,OK

* *Cymaenes odilia* (2) **Fawn-spotted Skipper** O,P,So
   o. trebius

Lerema accius (2,3,4) **Clouded Skipper** K,O,OK,P,So,S,TS
Grimy Skipper
White-spotted Brown Skipper
Accius Skipper H

Lerema liris (2) **Liris Skipper** O
Vettius fantasos (2) **Fantastic Skipper** O,So
* *Perichares philetes* (2) **Green-backed Skipper** O,P
Dolores Skipper K
Gaudy Skipper So
Confusing Brand Skipper

   p. adela
Rhinthon osca (2) **Osca Skipper** O
Decinea percosius (2) **Percosius Skipper** O
Decinea huasteca (2)

Conga chydaea (2) **Chydea Skipper** O
Ancyloxypha numitor (W) **Least Skipper** K,O,OK,S
Bordered Skipper
Least Skipperling M,P,So
Numitor Skipperling H
Numitor
Eastern Least Skipper

Ancyloxypha arene (2) **Tropical Least Skipper** K,O
Tropical Least Skipperling P,TS
Orange Least Skipperling So
Arene Skipper H
Arizona Yellow Skipper

Oarisma powesheik (1,3,C) **Poweshiek Skipperling** H,O,P
Poweshiek Skipper K,M,OK,TS
Parker's Broad Wing
Eastern Skipperling So
Iowa Dunn

Oarisma garita (1,2,C) **Garita Skipperling** H,O,P,TS
Western Skipperling So
Garita Skipper K,M,OK
Orange-tinted Broad Wing

Oarisma edwardsii (2)	**Edwards' Skipperling** H,P,TS
	Orange Skipperling So
Copaeodes aurantiacus (2)	**Orange Skipperling** H,K,O,OK,P,TS
	Hewitson's Skipper
	Western Tiny Skipper So
	Waco Skipper
Copaeodes minimus (2,4)	**Southern Skipperling** K,O,OK,P,TS
	Golden Skipper
	Tiny Skipper So
	Tiny Skipperling H
Adopaeoides prittwitzi (2)	**Sunrise Skipper** P
	Prittwitz's Skipper TS
	Black-veined Skipperling So
Thymelicus lineola (1,2,3,4,C)	**European Skipper** K,M,O,OK,P
	New English Skipper H
	European Skipperling So
Hylephila phyleus (W)	**Fiery Skipper** H,K,M,O,OK,P,So,S,TS
	Banded Skipper
	Bordered Skipper
	Great-headed Skipper
	Wedge-marked Skipper
p. muertovalle	
Yvretta rhesus (1,2,C)	**Rhesus Skipper** H,M,TS
	Plains Gray Skipper P
	Prairie Cobweb Skipper So
	Brown-banded Skipper
Yvretta carus (2)	**Carus Skipper** H,TS
	Desert Grey Skipper P
	Mexican Cobweb Skipper So
	Southwestern Skipper
c. subreticulata	Subreticulate Skipper TS
Pseudocopaeodes eunus (2)	**Eunus Skipper** H,TS
	Salt-grass Skipper P
	Alkali Skipper So
	Pale Yellow Skipper
e. wrightii	Wright's Skipper H
	Alkali Skipperling
e. alinea	
Stinga morrisoni (2)	**Morrison's Skipper** H,TS

	Morrison's Silver Spike P
	Arrowhead Skipper So
Hesperia uncas (1,2,C)	**Uncas Skipper** H,K,O,OK,P,TS
	White-vein Skipper So
u. lasus	Lasus Skipper H,TS
	Arizona Skipper
u. macswaini	MacSwain's Skipper TS
Hesperia juba (1,2,C)	**Juba Skipper** H,M,P
	Yuba Skipper TS
	Jagged-border Skipper So
* *Hesperia comma* (W)	**Common Branded Skipper** O,P
	Holarctic Grass Skipper So
	Comma Skipper M,TS
c. manitoba	Manitoba Skipper TS
	Canadian Skipper H,S
	Northern Skipper
c. assiniboia	Assiniboia Skipper TS
	Assiniboian Skipper H
c. laurentina	Laurentian Skipper K,OK
c. borealis	Labrador Skipper K
	Boreal Skipper TS
	Labrador Skipper K
c. harpalus	Harpalus Skipper TS
	Idaho Skipper H
	Orange-streaked Skipper
	Cabelus Skipper H
c. yosemite	Yosemite Skipper TS
c. leussleri	Leussler's Skipper TS
c. tildeni	Tilden's Skipper TS
c. dodgei	Dodge's Skipper TS
c. oregonia	Oregon Skipper H,TS
	Oregon Branded Skipper
c. hulbirti	Hulbirt's Skipper TS
	Hulbirt's Branded Skipper
c. ochracea	Ochraceous Skipper TS
	Ochre Skipper
c. colorado	Colorado Skipper H,TS
c. susanae	Susan's Skipper TS
c. oroplata	

Hesperia woodgatei (2)	**Apache Skipper** O,P
	Woodgate's Skipper H,TS
	Fall Skipper So
Hesperia ottoe (1,2,3,C)	**Ottoe Skipper** H,K,M,O,OK,P,TS
	Prairie Skipper So
	Plain Yellow Skipper
Hesperia leonardus (W)	**Leonard's Skipper** H,O,OK
	Leonardus Skipper K,M,P
	Leonard's Hesperid S
	Blazing Star Skipper So
l. pawnee	Pawnee Skipper H,K,O,P,TS
l. montana[T]	Montana Skipper
	Mountain Skipper H
	Pawnee Montane Skipper
Hesperia pahaska (1,2,C)	**Pahaska Skipper** M,O,OK,P,TS
	Yellow-dust Skipper So
p. williamsi	William's Skipper TS
p. martini	Martin's Skipper TS
Hesperia columbia (1,2)	**Columbian Skipper** H,P,TS
	Columbia Skipper
	Chaparral Skipper So
Hesperia metea (3,4,C)	**Cobweb Skipper** H,K,O,OK,P,So,S
	White-banded Skipper
m. licinus	Licinus Skipper H
	Homo Skipper
	Horus
Hesperia viridis (1,2)	**Green Skipper** H,K,O,P,TS
	Black-dust Skipper So
Hesperia attalus (1,2,3,4)	**Dotted Skipper** K,O,OK,P,So,S
	Wisconsin Skipper
	Attalus Skipper
a. slossonae	Seminole Skipper H
Hesperia meskei (2,4)	**Meske's Skipper** H,K,O,OK
	Dixie Skipper P
	Gulf Coast Skipper So
m. straton	
Hesperia dacotae (1,C)	**Dakota Skipper** H,K,O,OK,P,So,TS
	Skinner's Dakota Skipper
Hesperia lindseyi (1,2)	**Lindsey's Skipper** H,TS

Lindsey's Branded Skipper   P
Lost-egg Skipper   So
Hesperia sassacus (1,3,4,C)   **Indian Skipper**   K,M,O,OK,P, So,S
Sassacus Skipper   H
Pale-spotted Skipper
   s. manitoboides   Northwest Indian Skipper
Hesperia miriamae (2)   **Sierra Skipper**   P
Miriam's Skipper   TS
Alpine Skipper   So
Hesperia nevada (1,2,C)   **Nevada Skipper**   H,M,O,P,TS
Montane Skipper   So
Polites peckius (W)   **Peck's Skipper**   H,K,M,O,OK,TS
Yellow-spotted Skipper
Yellow Patch Skipper   P,So
Yellow Spot   S
Polites sabuleti (1,2,C)   **Sandhill Skipper**   H,P,TS
Salt-grass Skipper   So
   s. tecumseh   Tecumseh Skipper   H,TS
   s. chusca   Chusca Skipper   H
Arizona Skipper
   s. ministigma
   s. genoa
   s. alkaliensis
   s. albamontana
   s. sinemaculata
   s. basinensis
   s. nigrescens
Polites mardon (1)   **Mardon Skipper**   P,TS
Cascades Skipper   So
Washington Skipper
Little Oregon Skipper   H
Polites draco (1,2,C)   **Draco Skipper**   H,M,P,TS
Rocky Mountain Skipper   So
Dragon Skipper
Polites baracoa (4)   **Baracoa Skipper**   H,K,O,OK,P
Intermediate Skipper
Yellow Patch Skipper
Little Tawny Edge   So

Polites themistocles (W)	**Tawny-edged Skipper** H,K,M,O,OK,P, So,S,TS
	Fawn-edged Skipper
	Clear-winged Skipper
Polites origenes (1,2,3,4,C)	**Crossline Skipper** H,K,M,O,OK,P,So, S,TS
	Yellow-spotted Brown Skipper
o. rhena	Rhena Skipper H,TS
	Alcina Skipper H
Polites mystic (1,2,3,4,C)	**Long Dash** H,K,M,O,OK,P,So,S,TS
	Orange Skipper
m. dacotah	Dakotah Dash P
	Dakota Long Dash TS
Polites sonora (1,2,C)	**Sonora Skipper** H,M,P,TS
	Western Long Dash So
s. siris	Dog Star Skipper TS
	Siris Skipper H
s. utahensis	Utah Skipper TS
	Skinner's Utah Skipper H
Polites vibex (1,2,3,4)	**Whirlabout** K,OK,O,P,So,S,TS
	Geyer's Skipper H
v. praeceps	
v. brettoides	
Wallengrenia otho (2,3,4)	**Broken Dash** K,O,OK,P
	Red Broken Dash So
	Otho's Skipper H
	Yellow-brown Skipper
	Volcanic Skipper S
Wallengrenia egeremet (1,2,3,4,C)	**Northern Broken Dash** M,O,OK,P
	Volcanic Skipper
	Brown Broken Dash OK
	Immaculate Skipper
Pompeius verna (1,2,3,4,C)	**Little Glassywing** H,K,M,O,OK,P,So,S
	Vernal Skipper
	Spotted Skipper
	Dark Brown Skipper
	Glass-spotted Skipper
	Southern Little Glassywing
	Spotted Brown Skipper S

Atalopedes campestris (W)   **Sachem** H,K,M,O,OK,P,So,S,TS
                                     Field Skipper   TS
                                     Velvet-spotted Skipper
                                     Prairie Skipper

 c. huron
Atrytone arogos (1,2,3,4)   **Arogos Skipper** K,O,OK,TS
                                     Beard-grass Skipper   P
                                     Brown-rim Skipper   So

 a. iowa   Iowa Skipper   TS
                                     Arogos

Atrytone logan (W)   **Delaware Skipper** H,K,M,O,OK,P,TS
                                     Black-vein Skipper   So
                                     Yellow Skipper
                                     Vitellus Skipper

 l. lagus   Lagus Skipper   H,TS
Atrytone mazai (2)
Problema byssus (1,2,3,4)   **Byssus Skipper** H,K,O,OK,P
                                     Bunchgrass Skipper   P
                                     Golden Skipper   So

 b. kumskaka   Kumskaka Skipper   H
Problema bulenta (4)   **Rare Skipper** K,O,OK,P
                                     Golden Marsh Skipper   So
                                     Bulenta Skipper   H

Ochlodes sylvanoides (1,2,C)   **Woodland Skipper** H,M,P,TS
                                     Western Skipper   So
 s. pratincola   Meadow Skipper   H,TS
 s. napa   Napa Skipper   H,TS
                                     Allied Skipper

 s. santacruzus   Santa Cruz Island Skipper   TS
 s. orecoastus   Oregon Coast Skipper   TS
                                     Coastal Woodland Skipper

 s. bonnevillus   Bonneville Skipper   TS
Ochlodes agricola (1,2)   **Rural Skipper** P
                                     Farmer   TS
                                     California Skipper   So
                                     Field Skipper   H

 a. verus   Verus Skipper   H,TS
 a. nemorum   Forest Skipper   H
                                     Pacific Skipper

Ochlodes snowi (1,2)	**Snow's Skipper** H,P,TS
	Rusty Gully Skipper So
Ochlodes yuma (1,2)	**Yuma Skipper** H,P,TS
	Giant-reed Skipper So
Poanes massasoit (1,3,4,C)	**Mulberry Wing** H,K,M,O,OK,P,S
	Mulberry Marsh Skipper So
	Yellow Cross Skipper
m. chermocki	
Poanes hobomok (W)	**Hobomok Skipper** H,K,M,O,OK,P,S,TS
	Mormon S
	Northern Dimorphic Skipper So
	Orange and Brown Skipper
h. wetona	
Poanes zabulon (1,2,3,4,C)	**Zabulon Skipper** H,K,M,O,OK,P
	Southern Dimorphic Skipper So
	Yellow-fringed Brown Skipper
Poanes taxiles (1,2)	**Taxiles Skipper** H,O,TS
	Golden Skipper P
	Southern Dimorphic Skipper So
	Western Brown and Orange Skipper
Poanes aaroni (3,4)	**Aaron's Skipper** H,K,O,OK
	Saffron Skipper P
	Atlantic Marsh Skipper So
a. howardi	Howard's Skipper H
Poanes yehl (2,4)	**Yehl Skipper** K,O,OK,P
	Southern Swamp Skipper So
	Skinner's Skipper H
Poanes viator (1,2,3,4,C)	**Broad-winged Skipper** H,K,M,O,OK,P, S
	Broad Marsh Skipper So
	Viator Skipper
v. zizaniae	
Paratrytone melane (1,2)	**Umber Skipper** H,P,So,TS
m. vitellina	Vitelline Skipper TS
Choranthus radians (4?)	**Rayed Skipper**
	Lucas Skipper H
Choranthus haitensis (4?)	**Haitian V-mark Skipper**
	Haiti Skipper H
Choranthus vitellius (4?)	**V-mark Skipper**
Mellana eulogius (2)	**Eulogius Skipper** O

Mellana mexicana (2)

Euphyes arpa (2)   **Palmetto Skipper** O,OK,P,So
                                      Arpa Skipper H

Euphyes pilatka (2,3,4)   **Palatka Skipper** H,K,O
                                      Saw-grass Skipper OK,P
                                      Coastal Sedge Skipper So

Euphyes dion (1,2,3,4,C)   **Dion Skipper** H,K,O,OK
                                      Sedge Skipper P
                                      Eastern Sedge Skipper So

Euphyes bayensis (4)

Euphyes dukesi (2,3,4,C)   **Duke's Skipper** K,M,O,OK
                                      Scarce Swamp Skipper P
                                      Brown Sedge Skipper So

Euphyes conspicuus (1,2,3,4,C)   **Black Dash** K,M,O,OK,P,S
                                      Pontiac's Skipper H
                                      Great Lakes Sedge Skipper So
                                      Green-margined Skipper

  c. buchholzi

Euphyes berryi (4)   **Berry's Skipper** K,O,OK
                                      Florida Swamp Skipper P
                                      Florida Sedge Skipper So

Euphyes bimacula (1,2,3,4,C)   **Two-spotted Skipper** H,K,M,O,OK,
                                          P,TS
                                      Two-spot Sedge Skipper So
                                      Bright-rayed Skipper S

  b. illinois

Euphyes vestris (W)   **Dun Skipper** H,K,M,O,OK,P,S,TS
                                      Rustic Skipper
                                      Eastern Dun Skipper
                                      Immaculate Skipper
                                      Sedge Witch So
                                      Dun Sedge Skipper So
                                      Osceola Skipper H

  v. metacomet   Eastern Dun Skipper
                                      Dun Skipper M,OK,TS

  v. kiowah   Kiowa Skipper
  v. harbisoni

Asbolis capucinus (4)   **Monk** K,O,OK,P,So
                                      Palm Skipper So

Atrytonopsis hianna (1,2,3,4,C) **Dusted Skipper** H,K,O,OK,P,So,S,TS
Four-spotted Brown Skipper
h. turneri Turner's Skipper K
Atrytonopsis deva (2) **Deva Skipper** H,P,TS
Desert Dusted Skipper So
Atrytonopsis lunus (2) **Lunus Skipper** H,TS
Moon-marked Skipper P
Violet Dusted Skipper So
Atrytonopsis viereki (2) **Viereck's Skipper** H,P,TS
Four-corners Dusted Skipper So
Atrytonopsis loammi (4) **Loammi Skipper** H,K
Southern Dusted Skipper P
Dusted Skipper So
Atrytonopsis pittacus (2) **Pittacus Skipper** H,TS
Parchment Skipper P
White-bar Dusted Skipper So
Atrytonopsis python (2) **Python Skipper** H,P,TS
Yellowspot Dusted Skipper So
Margarita's Skipper
Atrytonopsis cestus (2) **Cestus Skipper** H,TS
Belted Skipper P
Baboquivari Dusted Skipper So
Atrytonopsis edwardsi (2) **Sheep Skipper** P
Ovinia Skipper TS
Rounded Dusted Skipper So
Edwards' Atrytonopsis H
Amblyscirtes simius (1,2,C) **Simius Roadside Skipper** K,M,TS
Orange Roadside Skipper P
Hilltop Little Skipper So
Simius Skipper H
Amblyscirtes exoteria (2) **Large Roadside Skipper** P,TS
Nanno Skipper H
Sonoran Little Skipper So
Amblyscirtes cassus (2) **Cassus Roadside Skipper** P,TS
Cassus Skipper H
Tawny Little Skipper So
Amblyscirtes aenus (2) **Bronze Roadside Skipper** K,O,P,TS
Aenus Skipper
Bronze Skipper H

Bronze Little Skipper So

Erna Roadside Skipper K,TS

Erna's Roadside Skipper

Amblyscirtes linda (2,4)   **Linda's Roadside Skipper** K,O,OK

Arkansas Roadside Skipper P

Amblyscirtes oslari (1,2,C)   **Oslar's Roadside Skipper** K,M,O,P,TS

Prairie Little Skipper So

Oslar Skipper

Oslar's Skipper H

Amblyscirtes elissa (2)

Amblyscirtes hegon (W)   **Pepper and Salt Skipper** H,K,M,O,OK,
P,So

Pepper and Salt S

Yellow-fringed Brown Skipper

Little Brown Skipper

Greenish Little Skipper So

Amblyscirtes texanae (2)   **Texas Roadside Skipper** K,P,TS

Southwest Little Skipper So

Amblyscirtes tolteca (2)   **Spotted Little Skipper** So

Amblyscirtes prenda (2)   **Prenda Roadside Skipper** P,TS

Spotted Little Skipper

Amblyscirtes aesculapius (2,4)   **Lace-winged Roadside Skipper** O,OK,P

Textor Skipper K

Woven-winged Skipper H

Eastern Brown Skipper

Cobweb Little Skipper So

Amblyscirtes carolina (2,4)   **Carolina Roadside Skipper** K,O,P,OK

Carolina Skipper H

Yellow Little Skipper So

Amblyscirtes reversa (2,4)   **Reversed Roadside Skipper** O,OK

Cane Little Skipper So

Amblyscirtes nereus (2)   **Slaty Roadside Skipper** P

Nereus Roadside Skipper TS

Nereus Skipper H

Creamy Little Skipper So

Amblyscirtes nysa (2)   **Nysa Roadside Skipper** K,O,OK,TS

Mottled Roadside Skipper P

Nysa Skipper H

Texas Brown Skipper

	Mottled Little Skipper So
	Mottled Skipper
Amblyscirtes eos (2)	**Eos Roadside Skipper** K,O,TS
	Dotted Roadside Skipper P
	Eos Brown Skipper
	Starry Little Skipper So
	Phylace Skipper H
	Eos Skipper
Amblyscirtes vialis (W)	**Roadside Skipper** H,K,M,O,OK,P,S,TS
	Two-spotted Brown Skipper
	Black Little Skipper So
Amblyscirtes celia (2)	**Celias' Roadside Skipper** K,O,OK
	Celia Skipper H
	Roadside Rambler P
	Creekside Little Skipper So
Amblyscirtes belli (2,4)	**Bell's Roadside Skipper** K,O,OK,P
Amblyscirtes alternata (2,4)	**Least Florida Skipper** K,O,OK
	Least Floridan Skipper H
	Blue-dusted Roadside Skipper P
	Dusky Little Skipper So
Amblyscirtes phylace (2)	**Phylace Roadside Skipper** TS
	Red-headed Roadside Skipper P
	Dark Brown Skipper
	Red-head Little Skipper So
Amblyscirtes fimbriata (2)	**Orange-edged Roadside Skipper** P
	Bellus Roadside Skipper H,TS
	Red-rim Little Skipper So
Lerodea eufala (W)	**Eufala Skipper** H,K,O,OK,P,TS
	Rice Leafroller
	Greenish-brown Skipper
	Gray Skipper So
Lerodea arabus (2)	**Violet-clouded Skipper** P
	Arabus Skipper H,TS
	Arizona Brown Skipper
	Blotchy Gray Skipper So
Lerodea dysaules (2)	**Olive-clouded Skipper** O,P
Oligoria maculata (2,4)	**Twin-spot Skipper** K,O,OK,P
	Twin-spotted Skipper
	Three-spot Skipper So

	Twin-spot H,S
Calpodes ethlius (2,3,4)	**Brazilian Skipper** H,K,O,OK,P,S,TS
	Canna Skipper So
	Canna Leafroller
	Large Brown Skipper
	Large Canna Leafroller
Panoquina panoquin (2,3,4)	**Salt Marsh Skipper** K,O,OK,P,So
	Panoquin Skipper H
Panoquina panoquinoides (2,4)	**Obscure Skipper** K,O,OK,P
	Panoquinoides Skipper H
	Skinner's Cane Skipper
	Beach Skipper So
Panoquina errans (2)	**Wandering Skipper** H,P,TS
	California Skipper
Panoquina ocola (2,3,4)	**Ocola Skipper** H,K,O,OK
	Long-winged Skipper P
	Edwards' Cane Skipper
	Long-wing Skipper So
Panoquina hecebolus (2)	**Hecebolus Skipper** O,K
	Russet Skipper P
Panoquina sylvicola (2)	**Sylvicola Skipper** K,O
	Sylvan Skipper TS
	Sugar Cane Skipper So
	Purple-washed Skipper P
Panoquina evansi (2)	**Evans' Skipper** O,P
	White-barred Skipper So
Nyctelius nyctelius (2)	**Nyctelius Skipper** K,O
	Violet-banded Skipper P
	Latreille's Cane Skipper
Thespieus macareus (2)	**Variegated Skipper** O
	Macareus Skipper H
Erionota thrax (H)	**Banana Skipper** So,TS

Subfamily **Megathyminae—Giant Skippers**

Tribe **Aegialini—Agave Borers**

Agathymus neumoegeni (2)	**Neumoegen's Giant Skipper** H
	Orange Giant Skipper P
	Neumoegen's Agave Borer TS
	Neumoegen's Moth Skipper

	Tawny Giant Skipper So
n. carlsbadensis	Carlsbad Agave Borer TS
n. florenceae	Florence's Agave Borer TS
n. judithae	Judith's Agave Borer TS
n. diabloensis	Diablo Mountains Agave Borer TS
n. mcalpinei	McAlpine's Agave Borer
Agathymus chisosensis (2)	**Tawny Giant Skipper** So
	Chisos Agave Borer TS
Agathymus aryxna (2)	**Aryxna Giant Skipper** P
	Aryxna Agave Borer TS
	Arizona Giant Skipper So
	Dyar's Giant Skipper H
Agathymus baueri (2)	**Yavapai Giant Skipper**
	Bauer's Skipper
	Bauer's Agave Borer TS
b. freemani	Freeman's Agave Borer TS
Agathymus evansi (2)	**Brigadier** P
	Evans' Agave Borer TS
	Huachuca Giant Skipper So
Agathymus mariae (2)	**Mary's Giant Skipper** H
	Pecos Giant Skipper P
	Marie's Agave Borer TS
	Lecheguilla Giant Skipper So
m. chinatiensis	Chinati Mountains Agave Borer TS
m. lajitaensis	Lajitas Agave Borer TS
m. rindgei	Rindge's Agave Borer TS
Agathymus gilberti (2)	**West Texas Giant Skipper** P
	Gilbert's Agave Borer TS
	West Texas Agave Skipper O
Agathymus remingtoni	Coahuila Giant Skipper So
Agathymus valverdiensis (2)	**Coahuila Giant Skipper** So
	Valverde Agave Borer
	Val Verde Agave Borer TS
Agathymus estellae (2)	Brown Bullet P
Agathymus stephensi (2)	**Stephen's Giant Skipper** H
	California Giant Skipper P,So
	Stephen's Skipper
	Stephens's Agave Borer TS
Agathymus polingi (2)	**Poling's Giant Skipper** H

	Amole Giant Skipper
	Little Giant Skipper So
	Poling's Agave Borer TS
Agathymus alliae (2)	**Mojave Giant Skipper** P
	Alliae Skipper
	Allie's Agave Borer TS
	Canyonlands Giant Skipper So

Tribe **Megathymini—Yucca Borers**

Megathymus yuccae (2,4)	**Yucca Skipper** K,O,So
	Yucca Giant Skipper P
	Giant Yucca Skipper OK
y. buchholzi	Florida Yucca Skipper
Megathymus coloradensis (1,2)	**Colorado Giant Skipper** H,P
	Colorado Yucca Borer
	Yucca Skipper So
	Colorado Yucca Skipper TS
	Common Giant Skipper
c. elidaensis	Elida Yucca Borer TS
c. navajo	Navajo Yucca Borer TS
c. browni	Brown's Yucca Borer TS
c. stallingsi	
c. reinthali	
c. martini	Martin's Yucca Borer TS
c. maudae	Maud's Yucca Borer TS
c. arizonae	Arizona Yucca Borer TS
c. albasuffusus	Whitish Yucca Borer TS
c. reubeni	Reuben's Yucca Borer TS
c. winkensis	Wink Yucca Borer TS
c. wilsonorum	
c. louiseae	Louise's Yucca Borer TS
c. kendalli	
Megathymus cofaqui (4)	**Cofaqui Skipper** H,K,O,OK
	Cofaqui Giant Skipper P
	Strecker's Moth Skipper
	Southern Yucca Skipper So
Megathymus harrisi (4)	**Harris' Skipper**
	Southern Yucca Skipper So
Megathymus streckeri (1,2)	**Strecker's Giant Skipper** H,O,P
	Strecker's Yucca Borer TS

	Strecker's Yucca Skipper
	Plains Yucca Skipper So
s. texanus	Giant Texas Skipper K
	White-rimmed Giant Skipper H
	Texanus Yucca Borer
	Texas Yucca Borer TS
s. leussleri	Leussler's Giant Skipper H
	Leussler's Yucca Borer
Megathymus ursus (2)	**Ursine Giant Skipper** P
	Ursus Yucca Borer TS
	Desert Yucca Skipper So
u. violae	Viola's Yucca Borer TS
u. deserti	Desert Yucca Borer TS
Stallingsia maculosa (2)	**Manfreda Giant Skipper** O,P,TS
	Aloe Skipper So
	Manfreda Borer
	Smith's Giant Skipper

Superfamily **PAPILIONOIDEA**

Family **PAPILIONIDAE—Parnassians and Swallowtails**

Subfamily **Parnassiinae—Parnassians**

Tribe **Parnassiini**

* Parnassius eversmanni (A,C)	**Eversmann's Parnassian** M,P,TS
	Eversmann's Parnassius H,P
	Yellow Apollo So
e. thor	Alaskan Parnassian
Parnassius clodius (1,2,C)	**Clodius Parnassian** P,TS
	Clodius Butterfly
	Clodius M
	American Apollo So
†*c.strohbeeni*	Strohbeen's Parnassian TS
c. sol	Sol Parnassian TS
c. baldur	Baldur Parnassian TS
	Lorquin's Parnassian
c. claudianus	Claudianus Parnassian TS

c. pseudogallatinus	False Gallatin Parnassian TS
c. incredibilis	Incredible Parnassian TS
c. altaurus	Altaurus Parnassian TS
	Dyar's Parnassian
c. gallatinus	Gallatin Parnassian TS
c. menetriesi	Menetries Parnassian TS
c. shepardi	Shepard's Parnassian
Parnassius phoebus (1,2,A,C)	**Phoebus' Parnassian** P,TS
	Small Apollo So,TS
	Parnassius Butterfly
	Smintheus Parnassian
p. behrii	Behr's Parnassian TS
p. sternitzkyi	Sternitsky's Parnassian TS
p. olympiannus	Olympian Parnassian TS
p. smintheus	Smintheus
	Smintheus Parnassian TS
	Common Parnassian M
	Colorado Parnassian
	Large Parnassian
	Xanthus Parnassian
p. montanulus	
p. sayii	Say's Parnassian TS
	Holland's Parnassian
p. pseudorotgeri	False Rotger's Parnassian TS
p. apricatus	Kodiak Parnassius
	Sunny Parnassian TS
p. golovinus	Golovin Bay Parnassian TS
	Golovin Parnassius
p. alaskensis	Alaskan Parnassian TS
p. elias	Mt. St. Elias Parnassian TS
p. yukonensis	Yukon Parnassian TS

Subfamily **Papilioninae—Swallowtails**

Tribe **Troidini**

* Parides eurimedes (2)	**Cattle Heart** O,So
e. mylotes	Mylotes Cattle Heart
Battus philenor (W)	**Pipe-vine Swallowtail** H,K,O,OK,P,So, TS
	Blue Swallowtail M,S

	Green Swallowtail
	Aristolochia
p. hirsuta	Hairy Swallowtail TS
	Hairy Pipe-vine Swallowtail
	Acauda Swallowtail H
Battus polydamas (2,4)	**Polydamus Swallowtail** K,O,P
	Gold Rim O,P,So
	Reef Butterfly
	Polydamus Butterfly H
	Polydamus Gold Rim
	Black Page
p. lucayus	Tailless Swallowtail
	Polydamus Swallowtail OK
Battus devilliers (4?)	**De Villiers' Swallowtail** H

Tribe **Leptocircini**

Eurytides marcellus (3,4,C)	**Zebra Swallowtail** Hw,K,M,O,OK,P,So,S
	Pawpaw Butterfly H
	Kite Swallowtail
	Ajax
Eurytides philolaus (2)	**Dark Zebra Swallowtail** O,P
	Dark Kite Swallowtail So
Eurytides celadon (4?)	**Celadon Swallowtail** H,O
	Cuban Kite Swallowtail So

Tribe **Papilionini**

* *Papilio polyxenes* (W)	**Black Swallowtail** K,M,O,So,S,TS
	Eastern Black Swallowtail P
	American Swallowtail So
	Common Eastern Swallowtail
	Eastern Swallowtail
p. asterius	Parsnip Swallowtail K
	Common American Swallowtail H
	Parsleyworm
	Celeryworm
	Common Eastern Swallowtail
	Carawayworm
p. coloro	Wright's Swallowtail TS
	Rudkin's Swallowtail
	Desert Swallowtail P

Papilio joanae (2,3)	**Joan's Swallowtail** O
	Missouri Woodland Swallowtail OK
	Ozark Swallowtail P
Papilio kahli (C)	**Kahli Swallowtail** P
(*P. polyxenes* × *P. machaon*)	Kahl's Swallowtail M,TS
	Western Swallowtail So
Papilio brevicauda (C)	**Short-tailed Swallowtail** K,M,O,P,So
	Newfoundland Swallowtail H
	Maritime Swallowtail P
b. gaspeensis	Gaspe Swallowtail
b. bretonensis	Cape Breton Swallowtail
Papilio bairdii (1,2,C)	**Baird's Swallowtail** H,O,P,TS
	Bruce's Swallowtail
	Western Black Swallowtail M,P
	Holland's Swallowtail
	Artemisia Swallowtail So
b. oregonius	Oregon Swallowtail H,M,P,TS
b. dodi	Cypress Hills Old World Swallowtail
	Dod's Swallowtail TS
Papilio machaon (A,C)	**Old World Swallowtail** K,M,O,P,TS
	Artemisia Swallowtail So
	Banded Swallowtail
m. aliaska	Alaskan Old World Swallowtail TS
	Alaskan Swallowtail H
m. hudsonianus	Hudsonian Old World Swallowtail
	Hudsonian Swallowtail TS
m. pikei	
Papilio xuthus (H)	**Asian Swallowtail** So
	Citrus Swallowtail H
	Xuthus Swallowtail TS
Papilio zelicaon (1,2,C)	**Anise Swallowtail** M,O,P
	Zelicaon Swallowtail H,TS
	Western Swallowtail So
	Western Parsely Swallowtail
z. nitra	Nitra Swallowtail H,TS
	Gothic Swallowtail
Papilio indra (1,2,C)	**Indra Swallowtail** H,P
	Short-tailed Black Swallowtail P
	Short-tailed Swallowtail TS

	Mountain Swallowtail
	Indra M
	Cliff Swallowtail So
i. minori	Minor's Swallowtail TS
i. pergamus	Edwards' Swallowtail TS
	Pergamus Swallowtail H,TS
i. kaibabensis	Grand Canyon Swallowtail TS
	Kaibab Swallowtail
i. fordi	Ford's Swallowtail TS
i. martini	Martin's Swallowtail TS
i. nevadensis	Nevada Swallowtail TS
i. phyllisae	Phyllis's Swallowtail TS
i. panamintensis	Panamint Swallowtail TS
*Heraclides thoas (2)	**Thoas Swallowtail** O,P
	King Swallowtail So
	Thoas Butterfly
	Yellow Emperor Swallowtail
t. autocles	Thoas Swallowtail H
	King Page
*t. oviedo	Oviedo Swallowtail
Heraclides cresphontes (W)	**Giant Swallowtail** H,K,M,O,OK,P,So,S, TS
	Orange Dog P
	Orange Puppy
*Heraclides aristodemus (4)	**Schaus' Swallowtail** P
	Island Swallowtail So
a. ponceanus[E]	Schaus' Swallowtail K,O,OK,P
	Ponceanus Swallowtail
*Heraclides andraemon (4)	**Andraemon Swallowtail**
	Bahamas Swallowtail So
a. bonhotei	Bahaman Swallowtail O,Ok
Heraclides ornythion (2)	**Ornythion Swallowtail** H,O,So
	King Ornythion Swallowtail
*Heraclides astyalus (2)	**Lycophron Swallowtail** O
	Astyalus Swallowtail So
a. pallas	Pallas Swallowtail
*Heraclides androgeus (4)	**Androgeus Swallowtail** O
	Queen Swallowtail So
	Queen Page

a. epidaurus	Androgeus Swallowtail OK
*Heraclides anchisiades (2)	**Anchisiades Swallowtail** O,So
	Ruby-spotted Swallowtail P
	Red-spotted Swallowtail So
	Orange Dog
a. idaeus	Idaeus Swallowtail
Heraclides pharnaces (2)	**Pharnaces Swallowtail** O
Pterourus glaucus (W)	**Tiger Swallowtail** H,K,M,O,OK,P,So,S
	Eastern Tiger Swallowtail TS
	Turnus Swallowtail
	Black Emperor Swallowtail
g. canadensis	Canadian Tiger Swallowtail O,TS
	Canadian Swallowtail
g. maynardi	Southern Tiger Swallowtail
g. arcticus	Arctic Swallowtail
	Arctic Tiger Swallowtail TS
Pterourus rutulus (1,2,3,C)	**Western Tiger Swallowtail** M,O,P,TS
	Western Swallowtail
	Rutulus Butterfly
	Tiger Swallowtail
	Pacific Tiger
r. arizonensis	Arizona Tiger Swallowtail TS
Pterourus multicaudatus (1,2,C)	**Two-tailed Swallowtail** M,O,TS
	Daunus Swallowtail
	Two-tailed Tiger Swallowtail P,So
	Daunus Butterfly H
	Three-tailed Swallowtail
	Daunus
Pterourus eurymedon (1,2,C)	**Pale Swallowtail** H,M,P,TS
	Pale Tiger Swallowtail P
	Pallid Tiger Swallowtail So
	Eurymedon Butterfly
	White Tiger Swallowtail
	White-striped Swallowtail
	Eurymedon
	Mountain Swallowtail
Pterourus pilumnus (2)	**Three-tailed Swallowtail** O
	Pilumnus Swallowtail H
	Three-tailed Tiger Swallowtail So

Pterourus troilus (W)	**Spicebush Swallowtail** H,Hw,K,O,OK, P,So,TS
	Green Clouded Swallowtail M,P,S
	Blue Swallowtail
	Mellow Bug
t. ilioneus	Coastal Spicebush Swallowtail
Pterourus palamedes (2,4)	**Palamedes Swallowtail** H,O,OK,P
	Magnolia Swallowtail
	Laurel Swallowtail So
Pterourus victorinus (2)	**Victorine Swallowtail** O

Family **PIERIDAE**—Whites and Sulphurs

Subfamily **Pierinae**—Whites

Tribe **Pierini**

Catasticta nimbice (2)	
Neophasia menapia (1,2,3,C)	**Pine White** H,Hw,M,O,OK,P,So,TS
	White Pine Butterfly
	Pine Butterfly
m. tau	White Pine Butterfly
m. melanica	Coastal Pine White TS
Neophasia terlootii (2)	**Chiricahua Pine White** P
	Terloot's White H
	Mexican Pine White So
	Southern Pine White TS
*Appias drusilla (2,3,4)	**Tropical White** O,So
	Florida White P
d. poeyi	Tropical White
	Caperwhite
d. neumoegeni	Florida White H,Hw,K,OK,P
Pontia beckerii (1,2,C)	**Becker's White** H,Hw,M,P,TS
	Sagebrush White
	Great Basin White So
Pontia sisymbrii (1,2,C)	**California White** H,M,P,TS
	Spring White P,So
	Sisymbrium White
s. flavitincta	Flavous White TS
s. elivata	Colorado White

	Sisymbrium White
	Alpine White TS
s. nordini	Nordin's White TS
Pontia protodice (W)	**Checkered White** Hw,K,M,O,OK,P,So,S, TS
	Common White H,P
	Southern Cabbageworm
	Southern Cabbage Butterfly
	Cabbage Butterfly
	Banded White Butterfly H
Pontia occidentalis (1,2,3,A,C)	**Western White** H,M,O,OK,P,TS
	Western Checkered White
	Western Cabbage Butterfly
	Checkered White
	Peak White So
o. nelsoni	Nelson's White M,TS
Pieris napi (W)	**Mustard White** H,K,O,P,TS
	Pot-herb Butterfly
	Mustard Butterfly
	Sharp-veined White So
	Veined White M,P
n. pseudobryoniae	Alaskan White
	Alaskan Mustard White TS
n. hulda	Coastal Alaskan White TS
n. frigida	Mustard Butterfly
n. oleracea	Grey-veined White S
	Mustard White O,OK
	Harris' White
	Veined White TS
	Pot-herb Butterfly
n. castoria	Reakirt's White
	Small-veined White
n. marginalis	Margined White M,TS
n. mcdunnoughi	McDunnough's White TS
	Veined White
n. mogollon	Mogollon White TS
Pieris virginiensis (3,4,C)	**West Virginia White** K,M,O,OK,P
	Diffuse-veined White So
	Toothwort White

Note: the asterisk precedes *Pieris napi* (W) as "* *Pieris napi* (W)".

	Edward's White Butterfly H
Pieris rapae (W)	**Cabbage Butterfly** H,Hw,M,O,P,So,S, TS
	European Cabbage Butterfly K,OK
	Cabbage White P
	European Small White
	Imported Cabbageworm
	Imported Cabbageworm Butterfly
	Imported Cabbage Butterfly
	Small White P,So
	Garden White Butterfly
	European Cabbage White P
	Imported Cabbage White
Ascia monuste (2,4,C)	**Great Southern White** H,K,O,P,TS
	Southern White So
	Gulf White
m. phileta	Great Southern White OK,TS
	Cabbage White
	Mustard White
m. cleomes	
Ganyra josephina (2)	**Giant White** K,O,P,So
	Josephine's White
	Amaryllis White H
j. josepha	Giant White TS

Subfamily **Anthocharinae—Marbles and Orange Tips**

Tribe **Anthocharini**

Euchloe ausonides (1,2,3,A,C)	**Large Marble** H,O,OK,TS
	Creamy Marble M
	Creamy Marble Wing P
	Ausonides
	Ausonides Marble
	Dappled Marble So
	Western Orange Tip
a. coloradensis	Colorado Marble TS
a. mayi	May's Marble TS
a. palaeoreios	Johnson's Marble TS
Euchloe creusa (1,A,C)	**Northern Marble** So
	Creusa Marble H,TS

	Creusa
	Northern Marble Wing P
Euchloe hyantis (1,2,C)	**Pearly Marble**
	Pearly Marble Wing P
	Hyantis Marble
	Edwards's Marble H,TS
	Edward's Marble Wing
	Western Marble So
h. andrewsi	Martin's Marble
	Andrew's Marble TS
h. lotta	Southern Marble H,TS
	Lotta Marble
Euchloe olympia (W)	**Olympia Marble** Hw,M,O,OK,TS
	Olympia K
	Olympian Marble
	Olympia Marble Wing P
	Rosy Marble H,So,TS
Anthocharis cethura (2)	**Felder's Orange Tip** TS
	Cethura
	Cethura Orange Tip H
	Desert Orange Tip P,So
c. catalina	Catalina Orange Tip TS
Anthocharis pima (2)	**Pima Orange Tip** H,P,TS
Anthocharis dammersi (2)	**Dammers' Orange Tip**
(*P. lanceolata* × *A. sara*)	
Anthocharis sara (1,2,A,C)	**Sara Orange Tip** M,P,TS
	Sara
	Sara's Orange Tip H
	Western Orange Tip So
	Lucas' Orange Tip
s. inghami	Ingham's Orange Tip TS
s. thoosa	Thoosa Orange Tip TS
s. julia	Colorado Orange Tip
	Julia Orange Tip TS
	Julia
s. browningi	Browning's Orange Tip TS
s. stella	Stella Orange Tip TS
	Stellar Orange Tip
	Stella

s. flora	Flora Orange Tip TS
s. alaskensis	Alaskan Orange Tip TS
Paramidea midea (W)	**Falcate Orange Tip** H,Hw,K,O,OK,P, So,S
	Orange Tip
m. annickae	Falcate Orange Tip
Paramidea lanceolata (1,2)	**Gray Marble** P
	Boisduval's Marble H,TS
	Lanceolate Marble
	Grinnell's Marble TS
	California White Tip So

Subfamily **Coliadinae—Sulphurs**

Tribe **Coliadini**

Colias philodice (W)	**Clouded Sulphur** Hw,K,O,OK,P,S,TS
	Common Sulphur H,K,M,P,So
	Yellow Clover Butterfly
	Roadside Sulphur
	Yellow Sulphur
	Mud Puddle Butterfly Hw
	Yellow Butterfly
p. vitabunda	Lively Clouded Sulphur TS
p. eriphyle	Western Common Sulphur
	Western Sulphur
	Common Yellow Sulphur
	Yellow Sulphur
	Western Clouded Sulphur TS
p. laurentina	
Colias eurytheme (W)	**Alfalfa Butterfly** K,O,OK,P,So
	Orange Sulphur K,M,OK,P,So,S,TS
	Alfalfa Sulphur
	Alfalfa Caterpillar
	Eurytheme
	Eurytheme Sulphur H
	Orange Clover Butterfly
	Roadside Sulphur
	Boisduval's Sulphur
Colias occidentalis (1,2,C)	**Western Sulphur** H,M,P,TS
	Golden Sulphur So
o. chrysomelas	Golden Sulphur

	Gold and black Sulphur H,TS
Colias alexandra (1,2,A,C)	**Queen Alexandra's Sulphur** M,P
	Queen Alexandra Sulphur TS
	Alexandra Sulphur H
	Alexandra's Sulphur O
	Ultraviolet Sulphur So
a. edwardsii	Edwards' Sulphur TS
	Henry Edwards' Sulphur H
a. columbiensis	Columbian Sulphur TS
a. astraea	Astraea Sulphur H,TS
a. christina	Christina Sulphur H,TS
a. krauthii	Krauth's Sulphur TS
a. kluanensis	Kluane Sulphur TS
a. apache	Apache Sulphur
a. harfordii	Harford's Sulphur H,TS
	Barbara Sulphur H
Colias pseudochristina (1)	**Intermountain Sulphur**
Colias meadii (1,2,C)	**Mead's Sulphur** H,M,P,TS
	Alpine Orange So
m. elis	Strecker's Sulphur H
	Elis Sulphur TS
m. lemhiensis	Lemhi Mountains Sulphur
Colias hecla (A,C)	**Hecla Sulphur** H,M,TS
	Greenland Sulphur P
	Hecla Orange K,M
	Arctic Sulphur
	Arctic Orange So
	Orange Arctic Sulphur O
h. hela	Hecla Sulphur TS
	Hecla Orange M
Colias canadensis (3,C)	**Canadian Sulphur**
	Arctic Orange So
Colias boothii (C)	**Booth's Sulphur** H,M,K,TS
(*C. hecla* × *C. nastes*; eastern form)	
Colias thula (C)	**Thula Sulphur** P,TS
(*C. hecla* × *C. nastes*; western form)	
Colias nastes (A,C)	**Labrador Sulphur** O,P
	Nastes Sulphur K,M,TS
	Arctic Sulphur

	Arctic Green Sulphur So
n. moina	Moina Sulphur TS
n. aliaska	Alaska Sulphur
	Alaskan Sulphur TS
n. streckeri	Strecker's Sulphur TS
Colias scudderii (1,2,A,C)	**Scudder's Sulphur** H,TS
	Scudder's Willow Sulphur P
	Willow Sulphur So
Colias gigantea (1,A,C)	**Giant Sulphur** K,M,O,TS
	Great Northern Sulphur P
	Large Willow Sulphur OK
g. harroweri	Harrower's Sulphur TS
Colias pelidne (1,A,C)	**Pelidne Sulphur** K,M,O,TS
	Labrador Sulphur H
	Blueberry Sulphur P,So
p. skinneri	Skinner's Sulphur H,TS
	Bean's Sulphur TS
Colias interior (1,3,C)	**Pink-edged Sulphur** H,Hw,K,M,O,OK, P,So,S,TS
Colias palaeno (A,C)	**Palaeno Sulphur** K,O,P,TS
p. chippewa	Palaeno Sulphur K,M,P,TS
	Chippewa Sulphur H
	Arctic Sulphur So
p. baffinensis	Baffin Island Sulphur
Colias behri (2)	**Behr's Sulphur** H,P,TS
	Sierra Sulphur P
	Sierra Green Sulphur So
Zerene eurydice (2)	**California Dog Face** Hw,O,P,So,TS
	Californian Dog Face H
	Western Dog Face
	Flying Pansy P
Zerene cesonia (2,3,4,C)	**Dog Face** K,M,O,OK,So
	Dog's Head Hw
	Southern Dog Face H,TS
	Dog's Head Butterfly Hw
	Poodle Butterfly
	Dog Face Butterfly P
	Black-based Yellow
Anteos clorinde (2)	**White Angled Sulphur** O,P

(Note: the asterisk * appears before *Colias palaeno* and *Anteos clorinde*.)

	Clorinde K,TS
	Clorinde Brimstone
	Ghost Brimstone So
	Yellow-spotted Gonatryx
	Giant Sulphur H
	Godart's Mammoth Sulphur
c. nivifera	Clorinde TS
Anteos maerula (1,2,4)	**Yellow Brimstone** O,So
	Yellow Angled Sulphur P
	Maerula K,TS
	Giant Brimstone OK
	Gonatryx
	Maerula Brimstone
Phoebis sennae (W)	**Cloudless Sulphur** K,M,O,So,TS
	Cloudless Giant Sulphur P
	Common Yellow
	Giant Sulphur
s. eubule	Cloudless Sulphur H,Hw,OK,S,TS
	Senna Sulphur
s. marcellina	Cloudless Sulphur TS
Phoebis philea (2,3,4)	**Orange-barred Sulphur** Hw,K,O,OK, So,TS
	Orange-barred Giant Sulphur P
	Red-barred Sulphur H,M
	Great Barred Sulphur
	Red-barred Giant Sulphur
	Jaune d'Abricot
Phoebis argante (2)	**Argante Giant Sulphur** O,P
	Argante Sulphur
	Apricot Sulphur So
	Apricot
	Orange Giant Sulphur
Phoebis agarithe (2,3,4)	**Large Orange Sulphur** H,K,O,So,TS
a. maxima	Cloudless Orange Sulphur
	Large Orange Sulphur OK
	Orange Giant Sulphur P
	Great Orange Sulphur
	Agarithe Giant Sulphur
Phoebis neocypris (2)	**Yellow Long-tailed Sulphur** O

Tailed Sulphur So
Giant Tailed Sulphur Hw
Tailed Giant Sulphur P

Aphrissa statira (2,4)   **Statira** K,O,P,TS
Yellow Migrant
Migrant Sulphur So

  s. jada   Cramer's Embossed-wing Sulphur
Statira TS

  s. floridensis   Migrant Sulphur
Yellow Migrant
Embossed-Wing Sulphur H
Statira Sulphur OK

Aphrissa orbis (4)   **Orbed Sulphur** O,OK,So
Kricogonia lyside (2,3,4)   **Lyside** H,K,O,OK,P,TS
Lyside Butterfly
Castalia K
Castalia Sulphur
Grey Sulphur
Lignum Vitae Yellow
Guayacan Sulphur So
Godart's Sulphur

Eurema daira (1,2,4)   **Barred Yellow** K,O,OK
Fairy Yellow H,K,P
Fairy Sulphur
Black-Banded Yellow
Black-Edged Sulphur
Delia H
Delia Sulphur
Barred Sulphur P,So

  d. palmira   Poey's Barred Sulphur
Palmira K

  d. lydia
Eurema boisduvalianum (2,4)   **Boisduval's Yellow** O,P
Boisduval's Sulphur K,OK,TS
Poodle Face Sulphur So

Eurema mexicanum (1,2,3,4,C) **Mexican Yellow** H,M,O,P
Mexican Sulphur K,OK,TS
Wolf Face Sulphur So

Eurema salome (2)   **Salome Yellow** O,P

	Salome Sulphur TS
	Monkey Face Sulphur So
s. limoneum	Salome Sulphur TS
Eurema proterpia (1,2)	**Tailed Orange** O,P,So
	Proterpia Sulphur TS
	Proterpia H
	Proterpia Orange K
	Tailed Sulphur Hw
	Jamaican Orange
	Gundlach's Sulphur H
	Gundlach's Orange TS
	Cadmium Orange
	Proterpia Yellow
Eurema lisa (2,3,4,C)	**Little Sulphur** H,K,M,OK,S,TS
	Little Yellow O,P
	Lisa Sulphur
	Lisa Yellow
	Little Sulphur So
Eurema chamberlaini (4?)	**Chamberlain's Sulphur** O,OK
	Bahamas Sulphur So
	Chamberlain's Yellow
Eurema nise (2,4)	**Jamaican Sulphur** OK
	Mimosa Yellow O,P
	Cramer's Little Sulphur
	Neda Sulphur
	Nise Sulphur K,TS
	Blacktip Sulphur So
n. nelphe	Nise Sulphur
Eurema messalina (4)	**Messalina Yellow**
m. blakei	Shy Sulphur O,OK
	Caribbean Dainty White P
* Eurema dina (2,4)	**Dina Yellow** O,P
	Dina Sulphur TS
	Bush Sulphur So
d. westwoodi	Westwood's Yellow H
	Dina Sulphur TS
	Dina Yellow
d. helios	Bush Sulphur OK
Eurema nicippe (W)	**Sleepy Orange** K,O,OK,P,TS

Sleepy Sulphur
Sleepy Orange Sulphur
Nicippe
Black-bordered Yellow S
Nicippe Sulphur H
Black-bordered Orange
Nicippe Yellow
Rambling Orange So
Small Orange

Nathalis iole (1,2,3,4,C)   **Dainty Sulphur** K,M,OK,P,So,TS
Dwarf Yellow H,O,P
Dainty Dwarf
Dainty Dwarf Sulphur
Yellow Dwarf

Subfamily **Dismorphiinae**

Enantia albania (2)   **Tropical Mimic White** O
Dimorphic Sulphur So

Family **LYCAENIDAE—Gossamer Wings**

Subfamily **Miletinae—Harvesters**

Tribe **Spalgini**

Feniseca tarquinius (W)   **Harvester** H,K,M,O,OK,P,So
Wanderer S
Piebald
Little Orange Butterfly
Brown-mottled Butterfly

    t. novascotiae

Subfamily **Lycaeninae—Coppers**

Tharsalea arota (1,2)   **Arota Copper** H
Arota
Tailed Copper P,So,TS
    a. virginiensis   Nevada Copper H
Virginia City Copper TS
    a. nubila   Cloudy Copper TS

	Tailed Copper
a. schellbachi	Schellbach's Copper TS
*Lycaena phlaeas (1,2,3,4,A,C)	**Little Copper** O,TS
	Small Copper M,So
p. americana	American Copper K,M,O,OK,P,TS
	Flame Copper P
	Small Copper
	Copper Butterfly
	Short-tailed Copper
p. feildeni	Feilden's Copper TS
	Arctic Copper H
	Tundra Copper
p. arethusa	Arethusa Copper TS
	American Copper
p. arctodon	Beartooth Copper TS
p. hypophlaeas	Western American Copper TS
	American Copper H,S
Lycaena cuprea (1,2,C)	**Lustrous Copper** H,M,P,So,TS
	Cupreus Copper
c. snowi	Snow's Copper H,P,TS
c. henryae	Henry's Copper TS
c. artemisia	
Gaeides xanthoides (1,2,3,A,C)	**Great Copper** H,M,TS
	Gray Copper So
	Great Gray Copper P
x. dione	Dione Copper H,O,TS
	Great Copper K,OK
Gaeides editha (1,2,C)	**Edith's Copper** H,P,TS
e. montana	Montana Copper TS
	Edith's Copper
e. nevadensis	
Gaeides gorgon (1,2)	**Gorgon Copper** H,P,TS
	Buckwheat Copper So
Hyllolycaena hyllus (W)	**Bronze Copper** H,K,M,O,OK,P,So,S,TS
	Large Copper
Chalceria rubida (1,2,C)	**Ruddy Copper** H,M,O,P,So,TS
r. duofacies	Idaho Copper TS
r. perkinsorum	Perkins' Copper TS
r. longi	Long's Copper TS

r. sirius	Sirius Copper H,TS
	Ruddy Copper
r. monachensis	Monache Copper TS
Chalceria ferrisi (2)	**Ferris's Copper** P,TS
Chalceria heteronea (1,2,C)	**Blue Copper** M,P,So
	Varied Blue H,TS
h. clara	Bright Blue H
	Bright Blue Copper TS
Epidemia epixanthe (3,C)	**Bog Copper** K,M,O,OK,P
	Cranberry-bog Copper So
	Least Copper
	Marsh Copper S
	Purple Disk S
	Epixanthe Butterfly
	Brown Copper
	Epixanthe Copper H
e. phaedra	Newfoundland Copper
e. michiganensis	
Epidemia dorcas (1,3,A,C)	**Dorcas Copper** H,K,M,O,OK,P,TS
	Cinquefoil Copper So
d. castro	Rocky Mountain Copper TS
d. florus	Florus Copper TS
	Purplish Copper
d. dospassosi	
d. claytoni	
d. megaloceras	Bighorn Copper TS
d. arcticus	Arctic Copper TS
Epidemia helloides (W)	**Purplish Copper** K,M,O,OK,P,So,TS
	Purple Copper
	Knotweed Butterfly
Epidemia nivalis (1,2,C)	**Nivalis Copper** P,TS
	Snowy Copper H,M
	Lilac-edged Copper So
	Lilac-bordered Copper P
	Pale Copper
n. browni	Brown's Copper TS
Epidemia mariposa (1,2,C)	**Reakirt's Copper** H
	Mariposa Copper M,P,TS
	Forest Copper So

	Dusky Copper
m. charlottensis	Queen Charlotte's Copper H
	Northern Copper TS
	Makah Copper
m. penroseae	Penrose's Copper TS
Hermelycaena hermes (2)	**Hermes Copper** P,TS
	Yellow Copper So

Subfamily **Theclinae—Hairstreaks**

Tribe **Theclini**

Hypaurotis crysalus (1,2)	**Colorado Hairstreak** H,P,So,TS
c. citima	Citima Hairstreak TS
Habrodais grunus (1,2)	**Boisduval's Hairstreak** H,TS
	Golden Hairstreak P
	Live Oak Hairstreak So
	Canyon Oak Hairstreak
	Chinquapin Hairstreak
g. lorquini	Lorquin's Hairstreak TS
g. herri	Herr's Hairstreak TS

Tribe **Eumaeini**

*Eumaeus atala	**Atala** K,O,OK,P
	Atala Hairstreak
	Coontie Hairstreak So
a. florida (3?,4)	Florida Blue-spot
	Florida Atala
Eumaeus toxea (2)	**Cycad Butterfly** O,P
	Mexican Cycad Hairstreak
	White-rim Cycad Hairstreak So
Atlides halesus (W)	**Great Purple Hairstreak** H,K,O,OK,P, TS
	Great Blue Hairstreak Hw,P
h. estesi	
Chlorostrymon maesites (4)	**Amethyst Hairstreak** O,P
	Verde Azul So
	Clench's Hairstreak
	Maesites Hairstreak K,OK
Chlorostrymon telea (2)	**Telea Hairstreak** H,O,P
Chlorostrymon simaethis (2,4)	**Simaethis Hairstreak** H,O,TS

	Silver-banded Hairstreak P,So
	Brown-margined Hairstreak
	St. Christopher's Hairstreak OK
s. sarita	Sarita Hairstreak K,TS
Phaeostrymon alcestis (2)	**Soapberry Hairstreak** O,P,So
	Alcestis Hairstreak H,K,OK,TS
a. oslari	Oslar's Hairstreak H,TS
Harkenclenus titus (W)	**Coral Hairstreak** H,M,O,OK,P,So,S,TS
	Little Brown Butterfly
	Mopsus Butterfly
	Cherry Tree Hairstreak
	Coral-streaked Butterfly
t. mopsus	Mopsus Butterfly
t. watsoni	Watson's Hairstreak TS
t. immaculosus	Immaculate Hairstreak TS
Satyrium behrii (1,2,C)	**Behr's Hairstreak** H,M,P,TS
	Orange Hairstreak
b. crossi	Cross's Hairstreak TS
b. columbia	Columbian Hairstreak TS
Satyrium fulginosum (1,2,C)	**Sooty Gossamer Wing** H,TS
	Sooty Hairstreak P,So
	Dusky Gossamer Wing
f. semiluna	Semiluna Hairstreak
	Semi-lunate Gossamer Wing
	Half Moon Hairstreak TS
Satyrium acadicum(W)	**Acadian Hairstreak** H,K,M,O,OK,P,S, TS
	Northern Willow Hairstreak So
	Pale Streaked Butterfly
a. coolinensis	Coolin Hairstreak TS
a. montanensis	Montana Hairstreak TS
a. watrini	Watrin's Hairstreak TS
Satyrium californicum (1,2,C)	**California Hairstreak** M,P,So,TS
	Californian Hairstreak H
	Western Hairstreak
Satyrium sylvinum (1,2,C)	**Sylvan Hairstreak** M,P,TS
	Western Willow Hairstreak So
s. dryope	Dryope Hairstreak H,TS
s. itys	Itys Hairstreak H,TS

s. desertorum	Desert Hairstreak TS
s. putnami	Putnam's Hairstreak H,TS
Satyrium edwardsii (W)	**Edwards' Hairstreak** H,M,K,O,OK,P,S
	Edwards' Streaked Butterfly
	Scrub-oak Hairstreak So
Satyrium calanus (W)	**Banded Hairstreak** H,K,M,O,OK,P,So, S,TS
	Florida Hairstreak
	Black Hairstreak
c. falacer	Falacer Hairstreak
c. godarti	Godart's Hairstreak TS
c. albidus	
Satyrium caryaevorum (3,4,C)	**Hickory Hairstreak** K,M,O,OK,P,So
Satyrium kingi (3,4)	**King's Hairstreak** O,OK,P
	Sweetleaf Hairstreak So
Satyrium liparops (W)	**Striped Hairstreak** H,K,M,O,OK,P,So, S,TS
	White-striped Hairstreak
	Ogeechee Brown Streak Butterfly
	Streaked Thecla
	White-bordered Streaked Butterfly
l. strigosum	
l. fletcheri	Fletcher's Hairstreak TS
l. aliparops	
Satyrium auretorum (2)	**Gold-hunter's Hairstreak** H,P,So,TS
	Golden Hairstreak
	Tacit Hairstreak H
a. spadix	Nut-brown Hairstreak H,TS
	Spadix Hairstreak
Satyrium tetra (1,2)	**Mountain Mahogany Hairsteak** P
	Gray Hairsteak H,TS
	Chaparral Hairstreak So
Satyrium saepium (1,2,C)	**Hedge-row Hairstreak** H,M,P,TS
	Buckthorn Hairstreak So
	Bronzed Hairstreak H,TS
	Nut-brown Hairstreak
	Russet Hairstreak
s. okanaganum	Okanagan Hairstreak TS
Ocaria ocrisia (2)	**Black Hairstreak** O,So

Ministrymon clytie (2)	**Clytie Hairstreak** H,K,O,P
	Silver-blue Hairstreak So
Ministrymon leda (2)	**Leda Hairstreak** H,P,TS
	Mesquite Hairstreak So
	Ines Hairstreak H,TS
Ministrymon azia (2,4)	**Azia Hairstreak** H,K,O,TS
	Tiny Hairstreak So
	Light-banded Hairstreak OK
Tmolus echion (2)	**Echion Hairstreak** O,TS
	Larger Lantana Butterfly P
	Four-spotted Hairstreak So
e. echiolus	Larger Lantana Butterfly TS
Siderus tephraeus (2)	**Tephraeus Hairstreak** O
Oenomaus ortygnus (2)	**Aquamarine Hairstreak** O,P
	Large Brilliant Hairstreak So
Rekoa zebina (2?)	**Zebina Hairstreak**
	Double-spotted Slate Hairstreak So
Rekoa spurina	**Spurina Hairstreak**
Rekoa palegon (2)	**Palegon Hairstreak** O
	Slated Hairstreak So
Allosmaitia pion (2)	**Blue-metal Hairstreak** So
Allosmaitia strophius (2)	**Strophius Hairstreak** O
Calycopis cecrops (2,4)	**Red-banded Hairstreak** H,P,O,OK,So
	Cecrops Hairstreak H
	Red-striped Hairstreak
Calycopis isobeon (2,4)	**Dusky-blue Hairstreak** O,P,So
	Beon Hairstreak K
	Dusty Blue Hairstreak OK
Callophrys dumetorum (1,2)	**Bramble Hairstreak** M,TS
	Bramble Green Hairstreak P
	Green White-spotted Hairstreak H
d. perplexa	Perplexing Hairstreak
d. oregonensis	Oregon Hairstreak TS
Callophrys comstocki (2)	**Comstock's Hairstreak**
	Comstock's Green Hairstreak TS
	Desert Green Hairstreak P
Callophrys lemberti (2)	**Lembert's Hairstreak** TS
	Alpine Green Hairstreak P
Callophrys apama (1,2)	**Apama Hairstreak** H,TS

Green Hairstreak
Canyon Green Hairstreak   P

a. homoperplexa
Callophrys affinis (1,2,C)   **Immaculate Green Hairstreak**   P
Affinis Green Hairstreak
Green-winged Hairstreak   H,TS
Green Hairstreak   M,So
a. washingtonia   Washington Hairstreak   TS
Washington Green Hairstreak
Green Hairstreak   M
Callophrys viridis (1,2)   **Green Hairstreak**   TS
Bluish-green Hairstreak   P
Coastal Green Hairstreak   So
Callophrys sheridanii (1,2,C)   **Sheridan's Hairstreak** H,M,TS
Little Green Hairstreak
Sheridan's Green Hairstreak
White-lined Green Hairstreak   P

s. neoperplexa
s. newcomeri   Newcomer's Hairstreak   TS
Cyanophrys miserabilis (2)   **Miserabilis Hairstreak**   O,P
Sad Green Hairstreak   So
Pastor Hairstreak   K
Morpho-blue Elfin   H
Cyanophrys goodsoni (2)   **Goodson's Hairstreak**   O,P
Silvery Green Hairstreak   So
Facuna Hairstreak
Cyanophrys herodotus (2)   **Tropical Green Hairstreak**   O,So
Mitoura spinetorum (1,2,C)   **Thicket Hairstreak**   M,P,TS
Blue Mistletoe Hairstreak   So

s. ninus
s. millerorum
Mitoura johnsoni (1,2,C)   **Johnson's Hairstreak**   H,M,P,TS
Mistletoe Hairstreak   P
Brown Mistletoe Hairstreak   So
Columbian Hairstreak
Mitoura rosneri (1,C)   **Rosner's Hairstreak**   M,TS
Plowfoot Hairstreak
Arborvitae Hairstreak
r. plicataria   Pleated Hairstreak   TS

Mitoura barryi (1)	**Barry's Hairstreak** P,TS
	Basin-and-range Hairstreak
b. acuminata	Acuminate Hairstreak TS
Mitoura byrnei (1,C)	**Byrne's Hairstreak** TS
Mitoura nelsoni (1,2)	**Nelson's Hairstreak** H,P,TS
	Incense Cedar Hairstreak P
n. muiri	Muir's Hairstreak P,TS
	John Muir's Hairstreak
Mitoura siva (1,2,C)	**Juniper Hairstreak** H,O,P
	Siva Hairstreak M,TS
s. juniperaria	Juniper Hairstreak TS
s. mansfieldi	Mansfield's Hairstreak TS
s. chalcosiva	Clench's Hairstreak TS
s. clenchi	
Mitoura loki (2)	**Skinner's Hairstreak** H,P,TS
	Loki Hairstreak P
Mitoura grynea (W)	**Olive Hairstreak** H,K,M,O,OK,P,S,TS
	Cedar Hairstreak So
	Green Hairstreak
	Auburn Thecla
	Green Streaked Butterfly
g. smilacis	Auburn Thecla
g. sweadneri	
g. castalis	Castalis Hairstreak
Mitoura hesseli (3,4)	**Hessel's Hairstreak** K,P,O,OK,
	White Cedar Hairstreak So
Mitoura thornei (2)	**Thorne's Hairstreak** TS
Xamia xami (2)	**Xami Hairstreak** H,K,O,P,TS
	Succulent Hairstreak So
x. texami	
Sandia mcfarlandi (2)	**Sandia Hairstreak** P
	Beargrass Hairstreak So
	McFarland's Hairstreak TS
	McFarland's Green Hairstreak
Incisalia augustinus (W)	**Brown Elfin** H,K,M,O,OK,P,So,S,TS
	Brown-streaked Butterfly
a. helenae	
a. croesoides	
a. iroides	Western Elfin H

	Western Brown Elfin TS
a. annetteae	Annette's Elfin TS
Incisalia fotis (2)	**Desert Elfin** So
	Fotis Hairstreak
	Early Elfin P
	Strecker's Elfin H,TS
	Arizona Gray Elfin
Incisalia mossi (1,2,C)	**Moss' Elfin** M,P
	Moss's Elfin TS
	Dr. Moss' Elfin H
	Stonecrop Elfin So
m. schryveri	Schryver's Elfin TS
m. bayensis[E]	San Bruno Elfin TS
	Bay Region Elfin
m. doudoroffi	Doudoroff's Elfin TS
m. windi	Wind's Elfin TS
	Wind's Hairstreak
Incisalia polia (W)	**Hoary Elfin** K,M,O,OK,P,So,TS
	Polios Elfin H
p. obscura	Obscure Elfin TS
Incisalia irus (W)	**Frosted Elfin** K,M,O,OK,P,So
	Hoary Elfin H,S
	Black Brown Hairstreak
	Swamp Brown Hairstreak
	Pearly-streaked Butterfly
i. arsace	
i. hadra	Hadros Elfin H
Incisalia henrici (W)	**Henry's Elfin** H,K,M,O,OK,P,TS
	Woodland Elfin So
h. margaretae	
h. solata	
h. turneri	
Incisalia lanoraieensis (3,C)	**Bog Elfin** K,M,O,OK,P
	Spruce-bog Elfin So
Incisalia niphon (W)	**Eastern Pine Elfin** O,P,So
	Eastern Banded Elfin TS
	Pine Elfin K,M,OK
	Banded Elfin H,S
	Brown Butterfly

	Niphon Butterfly
	Pine Hairstreak
	Black-and-white-banded Streaked Butterfly
n. clarki	Pine Elfin M
	Banded Elfin
Incisalia eryphon (W)	**Western Pine Elfin** M,O,P,So
	Western Banded Elfin OK,TS
	Eryphon H
	Marbled Elfin
e. sheltonensis	Shelton Elfin TS
	Shelton Pine Elfin
Arawacus jada (2)	**Jada Hairstreak** H
	Jade-blue Hairstreak P
	Nightshade Hairstreak
Fixsenia favonius (4)	**Southern Hairstreak** H,K,O,OK,P
	Southern Oak Hairstreak So
Fixsenia ontario (W)	**Northern Hairstreak** H,K,M,O,OK,P, S,TS
	Ontario Hairstreak
	Ontario Streaked Butterfly
o. autolycus	Autolycus Hairstreak TS
	Texas Hairstreak H
o. violae	Viola's Hairstreak TS
o. ilavia	Ilavia Hairstreak TS
Fixsenia polingi (2)	**Poling's Hairstreak** P,TS
	Rounded Oak Hairstreak So
p. organensis	
Hypostrymon critola (2)	**Sonoran Hairstreak** P
	Grizzled Hairstreak So
	Critola Hairstreak
Parrhasius m-album (W)	**White-M Hairstreak** H,K,O,OK,P,So,S
	Blue Hairstreak
Strymon melinus (W)	**Gray Hairstreak** K,O,M,OK,P,So,S
	Common Hairstreak H,P,TS
	Cotton Square Borer
	Bean Lycaenid
	Red-spotted Hairstreak
	Hop Vine Hairstreak
	Hop Butterfly

	Hop-eating Hairstreak
	Gray Streaked Butterfly
m. humuli	
m. franki	Frank's Common Hairstreak TS
m. pudicus	Common Hairstreak
	Modest Hairstreak TS
m. setonia	Seton Lake Hairstreak TS
m. atrofasciatus	Black-banded Hairstreak TS
Strymon avalona (2)	**Avalon Hairstreak** P,TS
	Catalina Hairstreak H,So
Strymon rufofuscus (2)	**Reddish Hairstreak** O,P
	Red-crescent Hairstreak So
Strymon bebrycia (2)	**Mexican Gray Hairstreak** O,P
	Balloon Vine Hairstreak So
Strymon martialis (4)	**Martial Hairstreak** H,K,O,P
	Long-tailed Hairstreak P
	Cuban Gray Hairstreak
	Blue-and-gray Hairstreak So
	Martialis Hairstreak OK
Strymon yojoa (2)	**Yojoa Hairstreak** O,P
	White-stripe Hairstreak So
* Strymon albatus (2)	**White Hairstreak** O,P,So
a. sedecia	
* Strymon acis (4)	**Acis Hairstreak** O,P
	Antillean Hairstreak So
	Drury's Hairstreak H
a. bartrami	Bartram's Hairstreak K,O,OK
Strymon alea (2)	**Lacey's Hairstreak** O,TS
	Alea Hairstreak P
	Tarugo Hairstreak So
* Strymon columella (2,4)	**Columella Haistreak** K,P,TS
	Dotted Hairstreak So
	Mallow Hairstreak O
c. modesta	Columella Hairstreak OK
c. cybira	Hewitson's Hairstreak
c. istapa	Columella Hairstreak TS
Strymon limenia (4)	**Disguised Hairstreak** O,OK,So
	Limenia Hairstreak P
Strymon cestri (2,H)	**Cestri Hairstreak** O,P

Spotted Hairstreak So

Strymon bazochii (2,H) **Bazochii Hairstreak** K,O,TS

Smaller Lantana Butterfly P

Mottled Hairstreak So

Gundlach's Hairstreak

Erora laeta (3,4,C) **Early Hairstreak** K,M,O,OK,P

Spring Beauty S

Blue-streaked Butterfly

Turquoise Hairstreak So

Erora quaderna (2) **Arizona Hairstreak** P

Quaderna Hairstreak TS

q. sanfordi Sanford's Hairstreak TS

Electrostrymon endymion (2) **Endymion Hairstreak** H,P

Ruddy Hairstreak So

e. cyphara Ruddy Hairstreak O

Electrostrymon angelia (4) **Fulvous Hairstreak** O,OK,So

Angelic Hairstreak P

Electrostrymon canus (2?) **Muted Hairstreak** O

Subfamily **Polyommatinae—Blues**

Tribe **Lampidini**

Brephidium exile (2) **Pygmy Blue** H,O,So,TS

Western Pygmy Blue Hw,K,OK,P

Boisduval's Pygmy Blue

Brephidium isophthalma (4) **Eastern Pygmy Blue** O,P

Dwarf Blue H

i. pseudofea Eastern Pygmy Blue Hw,K,OK

Lampides boeticus (H) **Long-tailed Blue** So,TS

Pea Blue

Bean Blue Hw

Bean Butterfly

Leptotes cassius (2,4) **Cassius Blue** K,O,OK,P

Tropical Striped Blue So

c. theonus West Indian Blue H

West Indian Banded Blue

Florida Banded Blue

c. striata Striated Blue Hw

Leptotes marina (1,2,3) **Marine Blue** H,Hw,K,O,OK,P,TS

Striped Blue So

	Marine Banded Blue
Zizula cyna (2)	**Cyna Blue** H,Hw,O,P,TS
	Tiny Blue So
	Imported Blue K
* Hemiargus thomasi (4)	**Caribbean Blue** O,So
	Thomas's Blue
	Miami Blue P
t. bethunebakeri	Miami Blue Hw,K,O,OK
* Hemiargus ceraunus (2,4)	**Ceraunus Blue** K,O,TS
	Southern Blue So
	Antillean Blue P
c. antibubastus	Ceraunus Blue OK
	Florida Blue H,Hw
	Filenus Blue
c. gyas	Edward's Blue
	Gyas Blue H,TS
c. zachaeina	Zachaeina Blue TS
* Hemiargus isola (1,2,3,4,C)	**Reakirt's Blue** H,Hw,K,O,OK,P,TS
	Solitary Blue P
	Mexican Blue So
	Isola Blue
i. alce	Reakirt's Blue M,P,TS

Tribe **Everini**

Everes comyntas (W)	**Eastern Tailed Blue** H,K,M,O,OK,P,TS
	Tailed Blue So,S
	Least Blue Butterfly
	Comyntas Butterfly
c. texana	Texas Tailed Blue TS
Everes amyntula (W)	**Western Tailed Blue** H,K,M,O,OK,P,So, TS
a. valeriae	Valerie's Tailed Blue TS
a. albrighti	Albright's Tailed Blue TS
a. herri	Herr's Tailed Blue TS

Tribe **Celastrini**

* Celastrina argiolus (W)	**Spring Azure** Hw,K,P,So,S,TS
	Common Blue
	Pale Azure
	Southern Azure

	Dotted Azure
	Pale Blue Butterfly
	Azure Blue
	Jenny Lind
a. ladon	Spring Azure M,O,OK,P,TS
	Common Blue
	Pale Azure
	Southern Azure
	Dotted Azure
	Pale Blue Butterfly
	Azure Blue
	Jenny Lind
a. lucia	Azure Butterfly
	Blue Lucia
	Common Blue TS
	Northern Azure Blue Hw
a. argentata	Fletcher's Blue TS
a. nigrescens	Dusky Blue
a. sidara	
a. echo	Echo Blue Hw,TS
	Echo Azure
	Southern Blue
a. gozora	
a. cinerea	Arizona Blue Hw
	Cinereous Blue TS
Celastrina ebenina (2,3,4)	**Dusky Azure** OK,P
	Sooty Azure P
	Spring Sooty So
	Dusky Blue O
Celastrina neglectamajor (3,4)	**Appalachian Blue** O,OK
Philotes sonorensis (2)	**Sonora Blue** H,Hw,P
	Sonoran Blue TS
	Stonecrop Blue So
Euphilotes battoides (1,2,C)	**Square-spotted Blue** H,Hw,M,P,TS
	Battoides Blue
	Buckwheat Blue So
	McDunnough's Blue
	Alpine Blue
b. centralis	Central Blue Hw,TS

b. ellisii	Ellis's Blue TS
b. glaucon	Glaucous Blue H,Hw,TS
	Glaucon Blue
b. oregonensis	Oregon Blue Hw,TS
b. baueri	Bauer's Blue TS
b. intermedia	Intermediate Blue Hw,TS
	Square-spotted Blue
	Bat Blue
b. martini	Martin's Blue Hw,TS
	Martin's Philotes
b. bernardino	Bernardino Blue,TS
	San Bernardino Blue Hw
b. comstocki	Comstock's Blue TS
b. allyni[E]	El Segundo Blue TS
	Allyn's Blue
Euphilotes enoptes (1,2,C)	**Dotted Blue** H,Hw,P,So,TS
	Enoptes Blue M
e. ancilla	Ancilla Blue Hw,TS
	Barnes' Blue
	Spotted Blue
e. columbiae	Columbian Blue TS
	Columbia Blue Hw
e. bayensis	Bay Region Blue TS
	Bay Blue Hw
e. smithi[E]	Smith's Blue Hw,TS
	Smith Blue
e. tildeni	Tilden's Blue Hw
e. langstoni	Langston's Blue TS
e. dammersi	Dammers' Blue TS
Euphilotes mojave (2)	**Mojave Blue** Hw,TS
	Mohave Blue H
Euphilotes rita (1,2)	**Rita Blue** H,Hw,P,TS
	Desert Buckwheat Blue So
r. coloradensis	Colorado Blue Hw,TS
r. emmeli	Emmel's Blue TS
r. mattonii	Mattoni's Blue TS
r. pallescens	Pallid Blue TS
	Pale Blue Hw,P
r. elvirae	Elvira's Blue TS

	Elvira Blue Hw
	Rita Blue
Euphilotes spaldingi (2)	**Spalding's Blue** H,Hw,TS
	Colorado Plateau Blue So
s. pinjuna	
Philotiella speciosa (2)	**Small Blue** H,Hw,P,So,TS
	Little Blue
s. bohartorum	Bohart's Blue TS
Vaga blackburni (H)	**Blackburn's Blue** P,TS
	Green Hawaian Blue So
	Hawaiian Blue P
	Blackburn Butterfly
Glaucopsyche piasus (1,2,C)	**Arrowhead Blue** H,M,P,So,TS
p. sagittigera	Southern Arrowhead Blue
	Coastal Arrowhead Blue
	Catalina Blue
	Cataline Blue Hw
p. nevada	Nevada Blue TS
p. daunia	Daunia Blue Hw,TS
p. toxeuma	Brown's Arrowhead Blue TS
Glaucopsyche lygdamus (W)	**Silvery Blue** H,Hw,K,M,O,OK,P,So,TS
	Appalachian Blue
l. mildredae	Mildred's Silvery Blue Hw
l. couperi	Couper's Blue H,TS
	Silver Blue S
	Northern Blue
l. afra	Afra Blue H,TS
l. jacki	Jack's Blue TS
	Jack's Silvery Blue Hw
l. oro	Oro Blue H,Hw,TS
	Silvery Blue
	Colorado Blue
l. arizonensis	Arizona Silvery Blue Hw,TS
l. australis	Southern Blue TS
l. incognita	Behr's Silvery Blue
	Behr's Blue TS
l. palosverdesensis[E]	Palos Verdes Blue
l. columbia	Skinner's Blue TS
	Columbia Blue H

	Columbia Silvery Blue Hw
†*Glaucopsyche xerces* (2)	**Xerces Blue** H,Hw,P,TS
	Eyed Blue H
*Lycaeides idas (W)	**Northern Blue** K,M,O,P,So,TS
i. anna	Anna Blue H,TS
	California Blue
i. ricei	Rice's Blue TS
	Anna Blue
i. lotis[E]	Lotis Blue H,TS
i. alaskensis	Alaskan Blue TS
i. scudderi	Scudder's Blue H,TS
	Pearl-studded Blue S
i. aster	Newfoundland Blue
	Aster Blue H
i. empetri	Crowberry Blue
i. ferniensis	Fernie Blue TS
i. atrapraetextus	Dark-edged Blue TS
i. sublivens	Dark Blue TS
i. longinus	Longinus Blue TS
i. nabokovi	Nabokov's Blue OK
Lycaeides melissa (W)	**Melissa Blue** K,M,O,OK,P,TS
	Orange-banded Blue H
	Orange-margined Blue So
	Orange-bordered Blue P
	Karner Blue M,OK,P
	Edwards' Blue
m. samuelis	Karner Blue
	Orange-bordered Blue
	Edwards' Blue
m. annetta	Annetta Blue H,TS
m. fridayi	Friday's Blue TS
m. paradoxa	Inyo Blue
	Orange-margined Blue TS
Plebejus saepiolus (W)	**Greenish Blue** H,M,O,P,TS
	Greenish Clover Blue So
	Saepiolus Blue K,OK
s. amica	Amica Blue H,TS
	Kodiak Blue H
	Glossy Blue

s. whitmeri	Whitmer's Blue TS
	Brown's Clover Blue Hw
s. gertschi	Gertsch's Blue TS
s. insulanus	Vancouver Island Blue TS
	Island Blue H
s. hilda	Hilda Blue H,Hw,TS
Plebulina emigdionis (2)	**San Emigdio Blue** H,Hw,P,TS
	Saltbush Blue So
Icaricia icarioides (1,2,C)	**Icarioides Blue**
	Common Blue P
	Lupine Blue So
	Boisduval's Blue H,TS
	Maricopa Blue H
i. pembina	Pembina Blue H,M,TS
	Manitoba Blue
	Silver Blue
i. lycea	Lycea Blue H,TS
	Boisduval's Blue
i. ardea	Ardea Blue H,TS
i. buchholzi	Buchholz's Blue TS
i. blackmorei	Blackmore's Blue H,M,TS
i. montis	Montis Blue TS
	Boisduval's Blue M
	Mountain Blue
i. pardalis	Pardalis Blue TS
	Puget Blue
i. pheres	Pheres Blue H,Hw,TS
i. missionensis[E]	Mission Blue Hw,P,TS
i. moroensis	Moro Blue TS
i. evius	Evius Blue TS
i. helios	Helios Blue
Icaricia shasta (1,2,C)	**Shasta Blue** H,M,P,TS
	Yosemite Blue
	Cushion-plant Blue So
s. minnehaha	Minnehaha Blue TS
	Shasta Blue
s. pitkinensis	Brown's Blue TS
	Alpine Blue
s. charlestonensis	

Icaricia acmon (1,2,3,C)	**Acmon Blue** H,K,M,O,OK,P,TS
	Emerald-studded Blue P
	Silver-studded Blue So
	Red-margined Blue
a. lutzi	Lutz's Blue TS
a. texana	Texas Blue TS
a. spangelatus	Spangled Blue TS
Icaricia lupini (1,2)	**Lupine Blue** P,TS
	Metallic-spotted Blue
	Large Silver-studded Blue So
l. monticola	Clemence's Blue TS
l. chlorina	Skinner's Blue TS
	Green Blue TS
Icaricia neurona (2)	**Veined Blue** H,TS
	Orange-veined Blue P
	Transvestite Blue So
Vacciniina optilete (A,C)	**Cranberry Blue** O,So,TS
o. yukona	Yukon Blue H,M,P
Agriades franklinii (A,C)	**Arctic Blue** K,O,P,TS
	High Mountain Blue P
	Labrador Blue H
	Primrose Blue So
	Franklin's Blue M
Agriades rusticus (1,2,C)	**Rustic Blue** H,TS
	Mountain Blue
	Rustic Arctic Blue
r. podarce	Gray Blue H,TS
	Arctic Blue
r. megalo	Large-spotted Blue TS
	Mountain Blue M
r. lacustris	Lake-side Blue TS
	Cascade Blue
	Precambrian Arctic Blue
r. bryanti	Bryant's Blue TS

Family **RIODINIDAE**—Metalmarks

Subfamily **Riodininae—Metalmarks**

Euselasia abreas (2?)

Calephelis virginiensis (3,4) **Little Metalmark** H,K,O,OK,P,So
Virginia Metalmark P
Louisiana Metalmark H

Calephelis borealis (3) **Northern Metalmark** H,K,O,OK,P,So
Large Metalmark S
Steel Speck

Calephelis nemesis (2) **Fatal Metalmark** K,O,P,TS
Dusky Metalmark H,P
Mexican Metalmark So

   n. australis Southern Metalmark H,TS
   n. dammersi Dammers' Metalmark TS
   n. californica California Metalmark
Dusky Metalmark TS

Calephelis perditalis (2) **Lost Metalmark** K,P,TS
Barnes' Metalmark H
Rounded Metalmark So

Calephelis wrighti (2) **Wright's Metalmark** H,P,TS
Sweetbush Metalmark So

Calephelis nilus (2) **Rounded Metalmark** O,So
Calephelis mutica (3,4) **Swamp Metalmark** K,O,OK,P,So
Calephelis rawsoni (2) **Rawson's Metalmark** K,O,P,TS
Southwest Metalmark So

Calephelis freemani (2) **Freeman's Metalmark** P,TS
Calephelis arizonensis (2) **Arizona Metalmark** TS
Calephelis dreisbachi (2) **Nogales Metalmark** P
Dreisbach's Metalmark TS

*Caria ino (2) **Red-bordered Metalmark** O,P
Schaus' Metalmark P

   i. melicerta Small Curvy Wing So
Domitian Metalmark K

*Lasaia sula (2) **Blue Metalmark** K,O,P,So
   s. peninsularis
Melanis pixe (2) **Pixie** O,P
Pixie Metalmark

Emesis zela (2)   **Zela Metalmark** P,TS
     Arizona Metalmark So
  z. *cleis*   Cleis Metalmark TS
     Cleis Butterfly
Emesis ares (2)   **Ares Metalmark** H,P,TS
     Chiricahua Metalmark So
     Ares Butterfly TS
Emesis emesia (2)   **Emesia Metalmark** K
     Falcate Metalmark P
     Big Curvy Wing So
     Curvy-wing Emesia O
Emesis tenedia (2)   **Falcate Emesia** O
Apodemia mormo (1,2,C)   **Mormon Metalmark** M,O,P,So,TS
     Mormon H
  m. langei[E]   Lange's Metalmark P,TS
  m. cythera   Cythera Metalmark H,TS
     Edwards' Metalmark
  m. duryi   Dury's Metalmark H,TS
  m. mejicana   Mexican Metalmark
  m. tuolumnensis   Tuolumne Metalmark TS
  m. virgulti   Behr's Metalmark H,TS
  m. deserti   Desert Metalmark TS
  m. dialeuca   Whitish Metalmark
Apodemia multiplaga (2)   **Narrow-winged Metalmark** O,P
     Pointed Metalmark So
     Schaus' Metalmark H
Apodemia hepburni (2)   **Hepburn's Metalmark** H,P,TS
Apodemia palmerii (2)   **Palmer's Metalmark** H,TS
     Gray Metalmark P
     Palmer's Mormon
     Mesquite Metalmark So
     Margined Metalmark
     Skinner's Metalmark H
Apodemia walkeri (2)   **Walker's Metalmark** K,O,P
     White Metalmark So
Apodemia phyciodoides (2)   **Crescent Metalmark** P
     Chiricahua Metalmark TS
     Crescentmark So
Apodemia nais (2)   **Nais Metalmark** H,P,TS

	The Many-spot Coppermark
	Coppermark So
Apodemia chisosensis (2)	**Chisos Metalmark** P,TS

Family **LIBYTHEIDAE—Snouts or Beaks**

Libytheana bachmanii (1,2,3,4,C)	**Snout Butterfly** H,K,M,P,So,TS
	Eastern Snout Hw
	Eastern Snout Butterfly OK
b. larvata	Southern Snout H
Libytheana carinenta (2,4)	**Tropical Snout** P
	Southern Snout P
	American Snout O
c. mexicana	Mexican Snout Butterfly
Libytheana motya (4?)	**Cuban Snout Butterfly**

Family **HELICONIIDAE—Longwings**

Subfamily **Heliconiinae**

Agraulis vanillae (1,2,3,4,C)	**Gulf Fritillary** H,K,O,OK,P,So,TS
v. nigrior	
v. incarnata	
Dione moneta (2)	**Mexican Silverspot** O,P
	Mexican Silver-spotted Fritillary So
m. poeyi	
Dryadula phaetusa (2,4)	**Banded Orange** O,So
Dryas iulia (2,4)	**Julia** K,P,O
	Iulia
i. largo	Orange Longwing OK,So
i. moderata	
Eueides isabella (2)	**Isabella Tiger** O,So
i. zorcaon	Isabella Tiger
Heliconius charitonius (2,4)	**Zebra** H,Hw,K,O,TS
	Yellow-barred Heliconian H
	Zebra Longwing So
	Zebra Butterfly
c. tuckeri	Zebra Longwing P

	Zebra OK
c. vazquezae	Zebra TS
Heliconius erato (2)	**Crimson-patched Longwing** O,P
	Red Passion Flower Butterfly So
e. petiveranus	

Family **NYMPHALIDAE—Brushfoots**

Subfamily **Argynninae—Fritillaries**

Euptoieta claudia (1,2,3,4,C)	**Variegated Fritillary** H,Hw,K,M,O,OK, P,So,TS
	Common Variegated Fritillary
	Pale Red Butterfly
Euptoieta hegesia (2)	**Mexican Fritillary** H,K,O,P,So
h. hoffmanni	
Speyeria diana (2,4)	**Diana** K,O,OK,P
	Diana Fritillary H
	Great Smokies Fritillary So
Speyeria cybele (W)	**Great Spangled Fritillary** H,K,M,O, OK,P,S,So,TS
	Cybele
	Yellow-banded Silver Wing
c. novascotiae	
c. krautwurmi	Krautwurm's Fritillary H
c. pseudocarpenteri	Chermocks' Fritillary TS
c. carpenterii	Carpenter's Fritillary H,TS
c. charlottii	Charlott's Fritillary TS
c. letona	Letona Fritillary TS
c. pugetensis	Puget Sound Fritillary TS
c. leto	Leto Fritillary H,TS
	Leto
	Western Silverspot
	Leto Silverspot
Speyeria aphrodite (W)	**Aphrodite Fritillary** H,M,O,OK,So
	Aphrodite K,P,TS
	Silverspot Fritillary S
	Silverspot
	Silver-winged Butterfly

	Venus Fritillary
	Venus's Argynne
a. winni	
a. alcestis	Ruddy Silverspot H
	Alcestis Fritillary TS
a. manitoba	Manitoba Fritillary TS
a. whitehousei	Whitehouse's Silverspot
	Whitehouse's Fritillary TS
a. columbia	Columbian Silverspot H
	Columbian Fritillary TS
a. ethne	New Mexican Silverspot H
	Ethne Fritillary TS
a. byblis	Byblis Fritillary TS
Speyeria idalia (W)	**Regal Fritillary** H,Hw,K,M,O,OK,P,S, So,TS
	Regal Silverspot Butterfly
	Regal Silver-wing
	Ideal Argynne
Speyeria nokomis (1,2)	**Nokomis Fritillary** H,P,TS
	Western Seep Fritillary So
	Nokomis
n. nitocris	Nitocris Fritillary H,TS
	Nitocris
n. coerulescens	Bluish Fritillary TS
	Mexican Fritillary H
n. apacheana	Apache Fritillary TS
Speyeria edwardsii (1,2,C)	**Edwards' Fritillary** H,M,O,P,TS
	Green Fritillary So
Speyeria coronis (1,2)	**Coronis Fritillary** H,M,O,So
	Crown Fritillary TS
	Coronis
	California Fritillary H
c. hennei	Henne's Fritillary TS
c. semiramis	Semiramis Fritillary TS
	Semiramis Silverspot H
	Semiramis
c. simaetha	Simaetha Fritillary TS
c. snyderi	Synder's Fritillary H,TS
c. halcyone	Halcyone Silverspot H

	Halcyone
	Halcyone Fritillary TS
Speyeria zerene (1,2,C)	**Zerene Fritillary** H,M,TS
	Zerene
z. *conchyliatus*	Royal Fritillary TS
z. *gloriosa*	Glorious Fritillary TS
z. *sordida*	Sordid Fritillary TS
z. *malcolmi*	Malcolm's Fritillary TS
z. *carolae*	Carol's Fritillary TS
z. *hippolyta*[T]	Hippolyta Fritillary H,TS
	Hippolyta
	Oregon Silverspot
z. *behrensii*	Behren's Fritillary H,TS
	Behren's Silverspot
	Behrens's Fritillary
z. *myrtleae*	Myrtle's Silverspot
	Myrtle's Fritillary TS
z. *bremnerii*	Bremner's Silverspot
	Bremner's Fritillary TS
	Valley Silverspot
z. *picta*	Painted Fritillary TS
	Ornate Silverspot
z. *garretti*	Garrett's Fritillary TS
z. *sinope*	Sinope Fritillary TS
z. *platina*	Skinner's Fritillary H
	Platina Fritillary TS
	Pfout's Fritillary TS
z. *gunderi*	Gunder's Fritillary TS
Speyeria callippe (1,2,C)	**Callippe Fritillary** M,O,P,So,TS
	Callippe
	Callippe Silverspot H
c. *comstocki*	Comstock's Fritillary TS
c. *liliana*	Liliana Silverspot H
	Liliana
	Lilian's Fritillary TS
c. *semivirida*	Green Silverspot
	Half-green Fritillary TS
c. *elaine*	Elaine's Fritillary TS
c. *rupestris*	Cliff-dwelling Fritillary H

	Rupestris Fritillary TS
c. juba	Yuba Fritillary TS
	Sierra Fritillary TS
	Plain Fritillary H,TS
c. laura	Laura's Fritillary TS
	Laura
c. nevadensis	Nevada Fritillary H,TS
	Nevada Silverspot
c. macaria	Macaria Fritillary TS
	Macaria H
	Macaria Silverspot
c. laurina	Unsilvered Macaria
	Unsilvered Macaria Fritillary TS
	Laurina Fritillary
c. harmonia	Mt. Wheeler Fritillary TS
c. meadii	Mead's Silverspot H
	Mead's Fritillary TS
c. gallatini	Gallatin Fritillary TS
c. calgariana	Calgary Fritillary TS
Speyeria egleis (1,2)	**Egleis Fritillary** H,P,TS
	Egleis
	Mountain Rambler H
	Montivaga H
	Great Basin Fritillary So
e. tehachapina	Tehachapi Fritillary TS
e. oweni	Owen's Fritillary TS
	Owen's Silverspot H
e. linda	Linda's Fritillary
	Linda Fritillary TS
e. macdunnoughi	McDunnough's Fritillary TS
e. albrighti	Albright's Fritillary TS
e. utahensis	Utah Fritillary TS
e. toiyabe	Toiyabe Fritillary TS
e. secreta	Secret Fritillary TS
e. moecki	
Speyeria adiaste (2)	**Adiaste Fritillary** H,P
	Adiaste
	Lesser Unsilvered Fritillary TS
	Unsilvered Fritillary

	Coast Fritillary So
a. clemencei	Clemence's Fritillary TS
a. atossa	Atossa
	Unsilvered Fritillary TS
	Atossa Fritillary H
Speyeria atlantis (W)	**Atlantis Fritillary** K,M,O,P,So,TS
	Mountain Silverspot H,OK,S
	Mountain Fritillary
	Mountain Silver-spotted Butterfly
a. canadensis	
a. hollandi	Holland's Fritillary TS
a. hesperis	Hesperis Fritillary H,TS
	Hesperis
a. nikias	Nikias Fritillary TS
a. dorothea	Dorothy's Fritillary TS
a. nausicaa	Arizona Silverspot H,Hw
	Nausicaa Fritillary TS
a. schellbachi	Schellbach's Fritillary TS
a. chitone	Chitone Fritillary H,TS
	Chitone
a. wasatchia	Wasatch Fritillary TS
a. greyi	Grey's Fritillary TS
a. tetonia	Teton Fritillary TS
a. viola	Viola's Fritillary
	Viola Fritillary TS
a. dodgei	Dodge's Fritillary TS
a. irene	Irene Fritillary H
	Irene's Fritillary TS
a. electa	Electa Silverspot H,TS
	Electa
	Electa Fritillary TS
	Cinnamon Silverspot
a. lurana	Lurana Fritillary TS
a. hutchinsi	Hutchins's Fritillary TS
a. beani	Bean's Fritillary H,TS
a. lais	Northwestern Silverspot
	Lais Fritillary TS
a. dennisi	Dennis' Fritillary TS
a. ratonensis	

a. elko
a. capitanensis
Speyeria hydaspe (1,2,C) **Hydaspe Fritillary** M,P,TS
Lavender Fritillary So

h. viridicornis Greenhorn Fritillary TS
h. purpurascens Purple Fritillary TS
h. minor Minor Fritillary TS
h. rhodope Rhodope Fritillary H,TS
Rhodope
Rhodope Silverspot
Dusky Silverspot

h. sakuntala Sakuntala Silverspot H
Sakuntala Fritillary TS

h. conquista New Mexico Fritillary TS
Speyeria mormonia (1,2,A,C) **Mormon Fritillary** H,M,O,OK,P,So,TS
Mormonia Fritillary
Mountain Fritillary

m. bischoffii Bischoff's Fritillary H,TS
m. opis Opis Fritillary H,TS
Opis
Caribou Silverspot

m. jesmondensis Jesmond Fritillary TS
m. washingtonia Washington Fritillary H,TS
m. erinna Erinna Fritillary H,TS
Alpine Fritillary

m. arge Mountain Rambler
Arge Fritillary TS

m. artonis Artonis Fritillary H
Artonis

m. eurynome Eurynome Silverspot H
Eurynome
Eurynome Fritillary TS
Clio Fritillary H
Clio

m. luski Lusk's Fritillary TS
*Boloria napaea (1,A,C) **Napaea Fritillary** M,O,P,TS
Mountain Fritillary So

n. alaskensis Alaskan Fritillary H,TS
n. nearctica Nearctic Fritillary TS

n. halli	Hall's Fritillary TS
* Clossiana eunomia (1,2,A,C)	**Bog Fritillary** K,M,O,OK,P,TS
	Huebner's Fritillary
	Arctic Fritillary
	Arctic Bog Fritillary
	Aphirape Fritillary
	Ocellate Bog Fritillary So
e. triclaris	Triclaris Fritillary H
e. alticola	Celestial Bog Fritillary TS
e. dawsoni	
e. nichollae	Mrs. Nicholl's Brenthis H
	Nicholl's Bog Fritillary
e. laddi	Ladd's Fritillary Hw
	Ladd's Bog Fritillary TS
e. ursadentis	Beartooth Bog Fritillary TS
e. denali	Denali Bog Fritillary TS
* Clossiana selene (W)	**Silver-bordered Fritillary** H,K,M,O,O K,P,S,TS
	Small Pearl-bordered Fritillary
	Silver Bog Fritillary
	Little Silverspot
	Pearl-bordered Fritillary
	Black-spotted Fritillary
	Silver Meadow Fritillary So
	Silver-bordered Butterfly
s. myrina	Myrina Butterfly
s. nebraskensis	Nebraska Fritillary TS
s. sabulocollis	Kohler's Fritillary TS
s. tollandensis	Tolland Fritillary TS
s. albequina	Whitehorse Fritillary TS
s. atrocostalis	Dark-bordered Fritillary TS
s. terraenovae	
Clossiana bellona (W)	**Meadow Fritillary** H,K,M,O,OK,P,S,So, TS
	Eastern Meadow Fritillary
	Brimstone Butterfly
	Bellona Butterfly
	Meadow Butterfly
b. toddi	Todd's Meadow Fritillary TS

	Meadow Fritillary K
b. jenistae	Jenista's Meadow Fritillary TS
* Clossiana frigga (1,2,3,A,C)	**Frigga's Fritillary** O,P,TS
	Frigga Fritillary H,M,OK
	Willow Bog Fritillary So
f. saga	Saga Fritillary K
	Labrador Fritillary
f. gibsoni	Gibson's Fritillary H
	Frigga's Fritillary TS
f. sagata	Sagata Fritillary TS
Clossiana improba (1,A,C)	**Dingy Arctic Fritillary** K,M,O,P
	Dusky-winged Fritillary
	Dingy Northern Fritillary TS
	Dark-winged Fritillary H
	Young's Fritillary H
	Alaskan Fritillary
	Young's Dingy Fritillary
	Young's Dingy Northern Fritillary TS
i. harryi	
Clossiana acrocnema (2)	**Uncompaghre Fritillary** P,TS
Clossiana kriemhild (1)	**Kriemhild Fritillary** H,P
	Strecker's Small Fritillary TS
	Relict Meadow Fritillary So
Clossiana epithore (1,2,C)	**Western Meadow Fritillary** H,M,P,So,TS
	Epithore
	Epithore Fritillary
e. chermocki	Chermock's Meadow Fritillary TS
e. uslui	Northern Meadow Fritillary TS
e. sierra	Sierra Meadow Fritillary TS
Clossiana polaris (A,C)	**Polaris Fritillary** K,M,O,P,TS
	Polar Fritillary H,So
p. stellata	
Clossiana freija (1,2,3,A,C)	**Freija Fritillary** K,O,OK
	Freya's Fritillary P
	Freija's Fritillary TS
	Freyja's Fritillary M
	Lapland Fritillary H
	Zig Zag Fritillary So
	Northern Fritillary

f. tarquinius	Northern Fritillary
	Tarquinius's Fritillary TS
f. natazhati	Natazhati Fritillary H
	Mt. Natazhat Fritillary TS
	Nabokov's Fritillary TS
	Pleistocene Fritillary So
f. browni	Brown's Fritillary TS
Clossiana alberta (1,C)	**Alberta Fritillary** H,M,P,TS
	Albertan Fritillary
	Alberta Alpine Fritillary So
	Alberta
Clossiana astarte (1,A,C)	**Astarte Fritillary** H,M,P,TS
	Alpine Fritillary
	Astarte
	Arctic Ridge Fritillary So
a. distincta	Distinct Fritillary H
a. tschukotkensis	
* *Clossiana titania* (1,2,3,A,C)	**Titania Fritillary** O,OK
	Titania's Fritillary P
	Titan's Fritillary
	Titian Fritillary
	Purple Lesser Fritillary K,TS
	Purple Bog Fritillary So
	Purple Arctic Fritillary M
t. boisduvalii	Boisduval's Fritillary
t. rainieri	Tacoma Fritillary
	Rainier Fritillary TS
t. grandis	Purple Lesser Fritillary
	Purple Fritillary TS
t. montinus	White Mountain Fritillary H
	Dappled Fritillary S
t. ingens	Large Purple Fritillary
	Purple Fritillary TS
t. helena	Helena Fritillary
	Helena
	Colorado Purple Fritillary TS
	Helena's Fritillary
* *Clossiana chariclea* (A,C)	**Arctic Fritillary** K,M,O,P,TS
	Chariclea Fritillary H

	Chariclea
	Boisduval's Fritillary
c. arctica	Arctic Fritillary M,TS
c. butleri	Butler's Fritillary H
	Butler's Arctic Fritillary TS

Subfamily **Melitaeinae—Checkerspots**

Tribe **Melitaeini**

Poladryas minuta (2)	**Dotted Checkerspot** O,P
	Smaller Checkerspot H,TS
	Beardtongue Checkerspot So
	Small Checkerspot
m. nympha	Arizona Checkerspot TS
	Nymph-like Crescentspot H
Poladryas arachne (1,2)	**Arachne Checkerspot** H,P,TS
a. monache	Monache Checkerspot TS
	Pola Checkerspot H
	Gila Checkerspot H
* *Thessalia theona* (2)	**Theona Checkerspot** O,P,TS
	Menetries Checkerspot H
	Mexican Checkerspot So
t. thekla	Thekla Checkerspot H,TS
t. bolli	Boll's Checkerspot H,Hw,TS
Thessalia chinatiensis (2)	**Chinati Checkerspot** Hw,P
	Tinkham's Checkerspot TS
	Lecheguilla Checkerspot So
Thessalia cyneas (2)	**Cyneas Checkerspot** H,Hw,P,TS
	Black Checkerspot So
Thessalia fulvia (1,2)	**Fulvia Checkerspot** H,Hw,O,P
	Fulvous Checkerspot TS
	Fulvia Crescent
f. coronado	
f. pariaensis	
Thessalia leanira (1,2)	**Leanira Checkerspot** H,P,TS
	California Checkerspot
	Paintbrush Checkerspot So
l. wrighti	Wright's Checkerspot H,Hw,TS
l. cerrita	Cerrita Checkerspot Hw,TS
l. alma	Alma Checkerspot Hw,TS

	Strecker's Checkerspot H
l. oregonensis	Oregon Leanira Checkerspot
	Oregon Checkerspot TS
l. daviesi	Davies' Checkerspot TS
	Davies's Leanira Checkerspot
Chlosyne californica (2)	**California Patch** Hw,P,TS,So
	Californian Patch H
* *Chlosyne lacinia* (1,2)	**Bordered Patch** O,P,TS
	Geyer's Patch Butterfly
	Sunflower Patch So
l. crocale	Crocale Patch H,Hw,TS
l. adjutrix	Adjutrix Patch H,HW
	Bordered Patch TS
	Scudder's Patch Butterfly K
	Scudder's Patched Butterfly
Chlosyne definita(2)	**Definite Patch** O,P
	Aaron's Checkerspot H,Hw,TS
	Coahuila Checkerspot So
Chlosyne endeis (2)	**Endeis Patch** H,Hw,O
Chlosyne erodyle (2)	**Erodyle Patch** H
Chlosyne janais (2)	**Janais Patch** Hw,O,P
	Crimson Patch H
	Giant Patch So
* *Chlosyne rosita* (2)	**Rosita Patch** O,P
	Rosy Patch So
r. browni	
Chlosyne ehrenbergi (2)	
Chlosyne melitaeoides (2)	
Chlosyne marina (2)	**Checkered Patch** O
Charidryas gorgone (W)	**Gorgone Checkerspot** K,O,OK,TS
	Gorgone Crescentspot H,P
	Gorgone Crescent Hw
	Huebner's Crescentspot
	Great Plains Checkerspot So
	Ismeria Checkerspot K
g. carlota	Carlota Checkerspot
	Carlota Crescent
	Carlota Crescentspot
Charidryas nycteis (W)	**Silvery Checkerspot** K,O,OK,TS

	Silver Crescent S
	Silvery Crescentspot P
	Silver Crescent Butterfly
	Nycteis Crescentspot H
	Nycetis Crescent HW
	Silver Crescentspot
	Silver Crescent
	Streamside Checkerspot So
	Nycteis Checkerspot M
n. drusius	Drusius Checkerspot Hw
	Dark Silvery Checkerspot TS
n. reversa	Chermock's Checkerspot Hw,TS
Charidryas harrisii (1,3,C)	**Harris' Checkerspot** H,Hw,K,M,O,OK,P
	Harris Checkerspot
	Harris's Butterfly S
	Eastern Checkerspot So
h. ligetti	
h. hanhami	Hanham's Crescentspot H
	Hanham's Checkerspot Hw
Charidryas palla (1,2,C)	**Northern Checkerspot** H,P,TS
	Pale Checkerspot
	Eremita Checkerspot
	Palla Checkerspot M
	Creamy Checkerspot So
p. whitneyi	Whitney's Checkerspot Hw,TS
p. vallismortis	Death Valley Checkerspot TS
	Panamint Checkerspot HW
p. calydon	Calydon Checkerspot H,Hw,TS
	Rocky Mountain Checkerspot
p. flavula	Flavid Checkerspot Hw,TS
	Flavula Checkerspot H
	Desert Checkerspot
p. sterope	Palouse Checkerspot Hw
	Sterope Checkerspot TS
Charidryas acastus (1,2,C)	**Acastus Checkerspot** H,Hw,M,O,TS
	Acasta Checkerspot
	Sagebrush Checkerspot P
	Acastus's Checkerspot
	Dorothy's Checkerspot Hw,TS

Charidryas neumoegeni (2)	**Neumoegen's Checkerspot** H,Hw,TS
	Desert Checkerspot P
n. sabina	Sabina Checkerspot Hw
	Sabino Canyon Checkerspot TS
Charidryas gabbii (2)	**Gabb's Checkerspot** H,Hw,P,TS
	Coast Checkerspot
	Pearly Checkerspot So
Charidryas damoetus (1,2,C)	**Damoetas Checkerspot** H,Hw,M,TS
	Rockslide Checkerspot P
	Alpine Checkerspot
	Pearly Checkerspot So
d. malcolmi	Malcolm's Checkerspot H,Hw,TS
Charidryas hoffmanni (1,2,C)	**Hoffmann's Checkerspot** H,Hw,M,TS
	Aster Checkerspot P
	Pacific Checkerspot So
h. segregata	Segregated Checkerspot TS
h. manchada	Manchada Checkerspot Hw,TS
Microtia elva (2)	**Elf** O,OK
	Bates' Elf H
	Elva TS
	Little Elf So
Dymasia dymas (2)	**Dymas Checkerspot** H,O,P,TS
	Tiny Checkerspot So
d. chara	Chara Checkerspot H,Hw,P,TS
d. imperialis	Imperial Valley Checkerspot Hw
	Imperial Checkerspot TS
* Texola elada (2)	**Elada Checkerspot** O,P,TS
	Tiny Checkerspot
	Small Checkerspot So
e. ulrica	Ulrica Checkerspot H
	Callina Checkerspot TS
e. perse	Perse Checkerspot H,TS
Anthanassa texana (2,4)	**Texan Crescent** H,Hw,O,P
	Texas Crescent K,So,TS
	Texan Crescentspot P
	Texan Anthanassa
t. seminole	Seminole Crescent O,OK
	Seminole
Anthanassa frisia (2,4)	**Cuban Crescent** Hw,K,O,OK,TS

	Cuban Crescentspot P
	Black Crescent So
Anthanassa ptolyca (2?)	**False Black Crescent** O,So
Anthanassa tulcis (2)	**Tulcis Crescent** O,TS
	Dotted Anthanassa H
	Tulcis Crescentspot
Phyciodes vesta (1,2)	**Vesta Crescent** H,K,O,TS
	Vesta Crescentspot P
	Mesquite Crescent So
Phyciodes phaon (1,2,4)	**Phaon Crescent** H,K,O,OK,TS
	Phaon Crescentspot P
	Mat Plant Crescent So
Phyciodes tharos (W)	**Pearl Crescent** H,Hw,K,M,O,OK,S,So
	Pearly Crescentspot P
	Pearly Crescent
	Pearl Crescentspot
	Pearly Crescent Fritillary
	Prairie Pearl Crescent
	Woodland Pearl Crescent
	Beautiful Crescentspot
	Pharos Butterfly
	Light-house Melitey
	Little Black-bordered Butterfly
	Drappled Melitaea
t. arcticus	Pearl Crescent Hw
	Arctic Pearl Crescent TS
t. distinctus	Distinct Crescent TS
t. pascoensis	Pasco Crescent Hw
	Pearl Crescentspot
	Orange Crescent So
	Northern Pearl Crescent OK,TS
	Pasco Pearl Crescent
Phyciodes batesii (1,3,4,C)	**Tawny Crescent** K,M,O,OK,S,TS
	Tawny Crescentspot P
	Bates' Crescentspot H,P
	Bates Checkerspot
	Bates Crescent Hw
	Bates Pearl Crescent
	Dark Crescent So

Phyciodes pratensis (1,2,A,C) **Field Crescent** Hw,M,O,So,TS
Field Crescentspot P
Meadow Crescentspot H
Meadow Crescent
p. montanus Mountain Crescent H,Hw,TS
p. camillus Camillus Crescent H,Hw,K,TS
Camillus Crescentspot
Camillus's Crescent
Rocky Mountain Crescent Hw
Phyciodes pictus (1,2) **Painted Crescent** Hw,K,O,So,TS
Painted Crescentspot H,P
Phyciodes orseis (1,2) **Orseis Crescent** H,Hw,TS
Orseis Crescentspot P
California Crescent
Long-wing Crescent So
o. herlani Sierra Nevada Crescent HW
Herlan's Crescent TS
Phyciodes pallidus (1,2,C) **Pale Crescent** M,So,TS
Pallid Crescent Hw
Pallid Crescentspot P
p. barnesi Barnes' Crescent Hw
Barnes Crescentspot H
Barnes's Pale Crescent TS
Phyciodes mylitta (1,2,C) **Mylitta Crescent** H,Hw,M,TS
Mylitta Crescentspot P
Small Crescent
Small Crescentspot
Thistle Crescent So
m. callina Arizona Crescent Hw,TS
Callina Checkerspot H
m. thebais Thebais Crescentspot H
Tegosa anieta (2)
  a. luka
Euphydryas gillettii (1,C) **Gillette's Checkerspot** H,M,P,TS
Yellowstone Checkerspot P,So
Euphydryas anicia (1,2,A,C) **Anicia Checkerspot** M,P,TS
Paintbrush Checkerspot P
Hewitson's Checkerspot H
California Checkerspot

a. alena	Alena Checkerspot H,Hw,TS
a. bakeri	Baker's Checkerspot Hw,TS
a. bernadetta	Leussler's Checkerspot H,TS
	Bernadetta's Checkerspot
a. capella	Capella Checkerspot H,TS
	Barnes Checkerspot Hw
a. carmentis	Benjamins's Checkerspot H
	Carmentis Checkerspot TS
a. chuskae	Chuskae Mountains Checkerspot TS
a. cloudcrofti	Cloudcroft Checkerspot TS
a. effi	Eff's Checkerspot Hw,TS
a. eurytion	Mead's Checkerspot H
	Eurytion Checkerspot TS
	Bruce's Checkerspot H
a. helvia	Scudder's Checkerspot H,Hw
	Helvia Checkerspot TS
	Anicia Checkerspot
a. hermosa	Handsome Checkerspot TS
	Hermosa Checkerspot Hw
a. hopfingeri	Hopfinger's Checkerspot Hw,TS
a. howlandi	Howland's Checkerspot Hw,TS
a. irelandi	Ireland's Checkerspot H
a. macyi	Macy's Checkerspot Hw,TS
a. magdalena	McDunnough's Checkerspot H
	Magdalena Checkerspot TS
a. maria	Skinner's Checkerspot H
	Maria's Checkerspot Hw,TS
a. morandi	Morand's Checkerspot H,Hw,TS
a. veazieae	Veazie's Checkerspot TS
	Veazey's Checkerspot
a. wheeleri	Wheeler's Checkerspot H,TS
a. windi	Wind's Checkerspot Hw,TS
Euphydryas chalcedona (1,2,A,C)	**Chalcedon Checkerspot** H,Hw,P,TS
	Common Checkerspot
	Western Checkerspot So
	Chalcedon H
	Cooper's Checkerspot Hw
	Chalcedony Checkerspot
c. colon	Colon Checkerspot M,P,TS

	Snowberry Checkerspot P
	Colon
	Edwards' Checkerspot
c. corralensis	Rock Corral Checkerspot
	Corral Checkerspot Hw,TS
c. dwinellei	Dwinelle's Checkerspot Hw
c. kingstonensis	Desert Mountain Checkerspot
	Kingston Checkerspot TS
c. klotsi	Klots's Checkerspot Hw
c. macglashanii	MacGlashan's Checkerspot H,HW,TS
	Truckee Checkerspot H
c. nevadensis	Nevada Checkerspot Hw,TS
c. olancha	Olancha Checkerspot H,Hw,TS
c. paradoxa	Western Checkerspot
	Contrary Checkerspot TS
c. perdiccas	Island Checkerspot
	Perdiccas Checkerspot H,TS
c. quino	Quino Checkerspot
	Behr's Checkerspot H,Hw
c. sierra	Sierra Checkerspot H,Hw,TS
c. sperryi	
c. wallacensis	Gunder's Checkerspot Hw
	Wallace Checkerspot TS
Euphydryas editha (1,2,C)	**Edith's Checkerspot** H,Hw,P,TS
	Editha Checkerspot
	Editha
	Edith Checkerspot
	Ridge Checkerspot So
e. alebarki	Alebark's Checkerspot TS
	Klots' Checkerspot
e. augusta	Augusta Checkerspot H
	Augustina Checkerspot TS
	Quino Checkerspot
e. aurilacus	Gunder's Checkerspot H
	Aurilacus Checkerspot Hw
	Gold Lake Checkerspot TS
e. baroni	Baron's Checkerspot H,Hw,TS
e. bayensis	Bay Region Checkerspot TS
	Bay Checkerspot Hw

	Coastal Checkerspot
e. beani	Bean's Checkerspot H,M,TS
	Alberta Checkerspot
e. colonia	Colonia Checkerspot H,Hw,TS
e. edithana	Edithana Checkerspot Hw
	Strand's Checkerspot TS
e. fridayi	
e. gunnisonensis	Gunnison Checkerspot TS
e. hutchinsi	Hutchin's Checkerspot
	Hutchins's Checkerspot TS
e. insularis	Island Checkerspot TS
e. lawrencei	Lawrence's Checkerspot Hw,TS
	Remington's Checkerspot
	Lehman's Checkerspot Hw
e. lehmani	Lehman Caves Checkerspot TS
e. monoensis	Mono Lake Checkerspot Hw
	Mono Checkerspot TS
e. nubigena	Cloud-born Checkerspot H,Hw,TS
e. rubicunda	Ruddy Checkerspot H,Hw,TS
e. taylori	Taylor's Checkerspot H,Hw,TS
	Whulge Checkerspot
e. wrighti	Wright's Euphydryas
e. luestherae	Luesther's Checkerspot TS
e. koreti	
Euphydryas phaeton (1,2,3,4,C)	**Baltimore** H,K,M,O,OK,P,S,So
	Baltimore Checkerspot Hw
	Black Checker
	Black Melitaea
	Balmony Butterfly
	Turtlehead Butterfly
	Baltimore Fritillary
	Red-bordered Butterfly
	Phaeton Melitey
p. ozarkae	Baltimore Checkerspot
	Ozark Checkerspot Hw

Subfamily **Nymphalinae—Anglewings**

Tribe **Nymphalini**

Polygonia interrogationis (W)	**Question Mark** Hw,K,M,O,OK,P,So,TS

	Violet Tip S
	Semicolon
	Question Sign H
	Interrogation
	Semicolon Vaness
Polygonia comma (W)	**Hop Merchant** Hw,K,O,OK,P,S,TS
	Comma H,Hw,M,O,OK
	Orange Comma
	Brown Comma
	White-C Butterfly
	Comma Anglewing So
	Comma Vaness
Polygonia satyrus (1,2,3,C)	**Satyr Anglewing** Hw,K,M,O,OK,P,TS
	Satyr H,O
	Wandering Comma S
	Hop Butterfly
	Brown Comma
	Golden Anglewing So
s. neomarsyas	Western Satyr Anglewing TS
Polygonia faunus (W)	**Green Comma** Hw,K,M,O,OK,P,S,So
	Faun H,TS
	Green Anglewing So
	Fawn
	Faunus Anglewing P
	Marbled Comma
	Cinnamon Butterfly
	Green-banded Comma
f. smythi	Smyth's Anglewing
f. rusticus	Rustic Anglewing TS
	Faun Anglewing
f. arcticus	Arctic Anglewing TS
f. hylas	Colorado Anglewing H,Hw,TS
Polygonia silvius	**Silvan Anglewing**
	Sylvan Anglewing TS
Polygonia zephyrus (1,2,3,C)	**Zephyr** H,Hw,P,TS
	Zephyr Anglewing M,P
	Zephyrus Anglewing
	Hoary Anglewing
	Hoary Comma

	Variegated Comma
	Gray Comma
	Gray Zephyr
Polygonia gracilis (3,A,C)	**Hoary Comma** M,O,OK,P,S,So,TS
	Hoary Anglewing So
	Graceful Anglewing H
	Brown-banded Comma
Polygonia oreas (1,2,C)	**Oreas Anglewing** K,M,P,TS
	Oread Anglewing H
	Dark Gray Comma
	Dark Gray Anglewing
	Oreas Comma
o. silenus	Silenus Anglewing H,TS
	Western Comma
	Silenus
Polygonia progne (W)	**Gray Comma** Hw,K,M,O,OK,P,S,TS
	Progne H
	Dark Gray Anglewing So
	Dark Gray Comma So
	Gray-winged Comma
	Spinous Currant Caterpillar
	Silver-L Butterfly
	Progne Vaness
	Currant Anglewing
	Silver-C Grapta
p. nigrozephyrus	Dark-Gray Comma So
*Nymphalis vaualbum (1,2,3,4,C)	**Compton Tortoise Shell** Hw,M,O,OK,P
	Compton's Tortoise Shell
	Compton Tortoise
	Comma Tortoise Shell So
	False Comma TS
v. j-album	Compton Tortoise, H,S
	Compton Tortoise Shell K,TS
	White-J Butterfly
	Large Tortoise Shell
	Comma Butterfly
	Many Colored Vaness
	J-Butterfly
	Watson's Tortoise Shell TS

Nymphalis californica (1,2,3,C)	**California Tortoise Shell** H,Hw,M,O, OK,P,TS
	Western Tortoise Shell So
c. herri	Herr's Tortoise Shell TS
Nymphalis antiopa (W)	**Mourning Cloak** H,Hw,K,M,O,OK,P,S, So,TS
	Camberwell Beauty H
	Yellow Edge
	Antiopa Butterfly
	Trauermantel
	Morio
	Willow Butterfly
	White-border
	Antiope Vaness
	Yellow Bordered Butterfly
	Grand Surprise
	Spiny Elm Caterpillar
a. hyperborea	Northern Mourning Cloak TS
Nymphalis urticae (3,C)	**Small Tortoise Shell** O
	European Small Tortoise Shell P
Aglais milberti (W)	**Milbert's Tortoise Shell** H,Hw,O,OK,P, TS
	American Tortoise Shell S
	Small Tortoise Shell M
	Forked Butterfly
	Milbert's Butterfly
	Nettle Tortoise Shell
	Red Empress
	Fire-rim Tortoise Shell So
	Milbert's Tortoise
m. furcillata	Western Milbert's Tortoise Shell TS
m. viola	
Vanessa virginiensis (W)	**American Painted Lady** Hw,K,M,O,OK, P,So,TS
	Painted Lady S
	Hunter's Butterfly H,P
	Virginia Lady P
	Scarce Painted Lady
	Hunter's Painted Lady

	Hunter's Cynthy
	Marbled Cynthia
Vanessa cardui (1,2,3,4,A,C)	**Painted Lady** H,HW,K,M,O,OK,P, So, TS
	Thistle Butterfly H,P
	Painted Beauty S
	Cosmopolite K,P
	Cosmopolitan OK
	Thistle Cynthy
	Cynthia of the Thistle
Vanessa annabella (1,2,C)	**West Coast Lady** H,Hw,M,O,P,TS
	Western Painted Lady So
	Western Lady
	Malva Butterfly
* *Vanessa atalanta* (W)	**Red Admiral** H,Hw,K,P,S,So,TS
	Alderman P
	Atalanta Butterfly
	Nettle Butterfly
	Atalanta Vaness
	Red Admirable
a. rubria	Red Admiral M,O,OK,TS
Vanessa tameamea (H)	**Kamehameha** Hw,P,TS
	Kamehameha Butterfly So
Hypanartia lethe (2)	**Orange Map Wing** So
	Lethe
	Orange-banded Red
	Lethe Nymph H

Tribe **Hypolimnini**

Hypolimnas misippus (4)	**Mimic** H,O,OK,P,So
Junonia coenia (1,2,3,4,C)	**Buckeye** H,Hw,M,O,OK,P,S,So,TS
	Peacock
	American Peacock
	Lavinia Butterfly
	Large-eyed Junonia
	Coenia Butterfly
	Peacock Butterfly TS
c. nigrosuffusa	Dark Peacock TS
	Dark Buckeye P
Junonia genoveva (4)	**Genoveva** H

	Black Mangrove Buckeye So
	Caribbean Buckeye OK
g. zonalis	Tropical Buckeye So
Junonia evarete (2,4)	**West Indian Buckeye** P
	Florida Buckeye P
	Buckeye
	Smoky Buckeye So
	Lavinia H
	Caribbean Buckeye So
	Mangrove Buckeye O
Anartia jatrophae (2,4)	**White Peacock** H,Hw,K,O,P,So,TS
j. guantanamo	White Peacock OK,TS
j. luteipicta	White Peacock TS
Anartia chrysopelea (4)	**Caribbean Peacock** O,OK,So
	Huebner's Anartia
Anartia fatima (2,4)	**Fatima** K,O,P,So
	Brown Peacock
Siproeta stelenes (2,4)	**Malachite** Hw,O,OK,P,So
	Pearly Malachite H
s. biplagiata	Malachite

Subfamily **Limenitidinae—Admirals**

Tribe **Limenitidini**

Basilarchia arthemis (W)	**White Admiral** K,O,OK,P,So,TS
	Banded Purple H,K,M,P,S
	White-banded Butterfly
	Sylvan Basilarchia
	Circled Emperor
	Banded Emperor
	Artemis Limenite
a. rubrofasciata	Banded Purple
	White Admiral O
	Northern White Admiral TS
	Northern Emperor
a. astyanax	Red-spotted Purple H,Hw,K,O,OK,P,S, So,TS
	Ursula Butterfly
	Black Admiral
	Blue Victory

	Orange-spotted Butterfly
	Blue-banded Butterfly
	Ephestion Butterfly
	Wildcherry Limenite
	Gooseberry Butterfly
	Red-spotted Emperor
a. arizonensis	Arizona Admiral
	Arizona Red-spotted Purple TS
Basilarchia archippus (W)	**Viceroy** H,Hw,K,M,O,OK,P,S,So,TS
	Mimic K
	Disippus Butterfly
	Disippe Butterfly
	Brown Viceroy
	Misippus Butterfly
	Strip-footed Limenite
	Dark Veinlet
	Banded Red Butterfly
a. floridensis	Florida Admiral H
	Vice-reine
a. watsoni	Watson's Viceroy TS
a. obsoleta	Arizona Viceroy
	Western Viceroy TS
	Hulst's Admiral
	Western Admiral
a. lahontani	Nevada Viceroy TS
Basilarchia weidemeyerii (1,2,C)	**Weidemeyer's Admiral** H,Hw,M,O,P,TS
	Weidemeyer Admiral
	Western Admiral So
w. oberfoelli	Oberfoell's Admiral
w. latifascia	Wide-banded Admiral TS
w. nevadae	Nevada Admiral TS
w. angustifascia	Narrow-banded Admiral TS
w. siennafascia	
Basilarchia lorquini (1,2,C)	**Lorquin's Admiral** H,Hw,M,P,TS
	Orange-tip Admiral So
	White Admiral
l. burrisoni	Burrison's Admiral TS
	Lorquin's Admiral
	White Admiral

Adelpha fessonia (2)	**Mexican Sister** O,P,So
Adelpha bredowii (1,2)	**California Sister** O,P
	Sister So,TS
	Californian Sister H
	Sisters
	Bredow's Sister
b. eulalia	Arizona Sister TS
b. californica	California Sister TS

Tribe **Epicaliini**

Epiphile adrasta (2)	**Dimorphic Bark Wing** O,So
Myscelia ethusa (2)	**Blue Wing** P
	Blue Wave O,So
	Boisduval's Ethusa H
* Mycelia cyananthe (2)	**Cyananthe Blue Wing**
	Dark Blue Wave So
	Dark Wave
c. skinneri	Mengel's Mycelia H
Eunica monima (2,4)	**Dingy Purple Wing** H,K,O,OK,P,So
	Dingy Eunica
* Eunica tatila (2,4)	**Florida Purple Wing** H,K,P
	Purple Eunica
	Large Purple Wing O,So
	Mexican Purple Wing
t. tatilista	Florida Purple Wing OK
	Large Purple Wing
Dynamine mylitta (2)	**Mylitta Green Wing** P
Dynamine dyonis (2)	**Blue-eyed Green Wing** O,So
	Dyonis Green Wing P
	Mexican Dynamine H
Diaethria clymena (4?)	**Eighty-eight Butterfly** O,P,So
	Leopard-spot H
Diaethria asteria (2)	**Mexican Eighty-eight Butterfly O,So**
	Leopard-spot P

Tribe **Eurytelini**

Mestra amymone (1,2)	**Amymone** H,K,O,P,TS
	Texas Bagvein OK,So
	Noseburn Wanderer So
	Amymone Butterfly

* Mestra cana (4?)	**St. Lucie Mestra**
* Biblis hyperia (2)	**Red Rim** O,So
	Crimson-banded Black P
	Hyperia TS
h. aganisa	Hyperia

Tribe **Ageroniini—Crackers or Calicos**

* Hamadryas februa (2)	**Gray Cracker** O,So
	Gray-skirted Calico
	Haitian Cracker
f. ferentina	Ferentina Calico P
* Hamadryas amphichloe (4)	**Pale Cracker** O,So
a. diasia	
* Hamadryas atlantis (2)	**Dusky Cracker** So
a. lelaps	
* Hamadryas feronia (2)	**Blue Cracker** So
	White-skirted Calico H
	Cracker
f. farinulenta	
* Hamadryas guatemalena (2)	**Central American Cracker** O,So
	Guatemalan Calico P
g. marmarice	
* Hamadryas iphthime (2)	**Ringless Blue Cracker** O,So
i. joannae	
* Hamadryas amphinome (2)	**Red Cracker** O,So
	King Cracker
a. mexicana	

Tribe **Coloburini**

Historis odius (2)	**Stinky Leaf Wing** O,So
	Great Nymph H
	Orion
* Historis acheronta (2)	**Dash-wing** H
a. cadmus	Cadmus
Smyrna karwinskii (2)	**Karwinski's Beauty** H,P
	Nettle Bark Wing So
Smyrna blomfildia (2)	**Blomfild's Beauty** O,P

Subfamily **Marpesiinae—Dagger Wings**

Marpesia coresia (2)	**Waiter** O,P,So

Marpesia chiron (2,4)	**Many-banded Dagger Wing** H,O,TS
	Banded Dagger Wing P,So
	Common Dagger Tail
Marpesia petreus (2,4)	**Ruddy Dagger Wing** H,K,O,OK,P,TS
	Southern Dagger Tail
	Red Dagger Wing So
Marpesia eleuchea (4)	**Antillean Dagger Wing** O,So
	Cuban Dagger Wing OK
	Cuban Dagger Tail

Family APATURIDAE—Goatweed and Hackberry Butterflies

Subfamily Charaxinae—Goatweed Butterflies

Anaea aidea (2)	**Tropical Leaf Wing** K,O,P,TS
	Morrison's Tropical Leaf Wing TS
	Goatweed Butterfly H
	Leaf Wing So
	Eyed Goatweed
Anaea floridalis (4)	**Florida Leaf Wing** K,O,OK,P
	Leaf Wing So
	Florida Goatweed Butterfly P
Anaea andria (W)	**Goatweed Butterfly** H,K,O,OK,P,So,TS
	Goatweed Emperor
	Arizona Goatweed Butterfly
Memphis glycerium (2)	**Angled Leaf Wing** O,So
	Crinkled Leafwing P
Memphis pithyusa (2)	**Blue Leaf Wing** O,P,So
Memphis echemus (2?)	**Chestnut Leaf Butterfly** O

Subfamily Apaturinae—Hackberry Butterflies

Asterocampa celtis (W)	**Hackberry Butterfly** H,K,M,O,OK,P, So,TS
	Gray Emperor
	Hackberry Emperor P
	Eyed Emperor
	Empress Alicia H,P
	Alicia
	Buff Emperor

c. reinthali	
c. antonia	Antonia
	Empress Antonia H,P
	Antonia's Hackberry Butterfly TS
	Mountain Emperor H,P
	Mountain Hackberry Butterfly TS
Asterocampa leilia (2)	**Empress Leilia H,O,P,TS**
	Leilia K
	Desert Hackberry Butterfly So
	Cocles's Emperor TS
Asterocampa clyton (W)	**Tawny Emperor H,Hw,K,M,O,OK,P,S, So,TS**
	Brown Emperor
	Tawny Hackberry
c. flora	Empress Flora H,P
	Flora
	Red Emperor
c. texana	Texan Emperor
	Texas Emperor P
	Texas Tawny Emperor TS
	Pale Emperor P
	Pallid Emperor TS
	Skinner's Hackberry Butterfly H
c. louisa	Empress Louisa P
Doxocopa pavon (2)	**Pavon O,P**
	Purple Emperor So
Doxocopa laure (2)	**Laure O,P**
	Silver Emperor So
	Cuban Emperor

Family SATYRIDAE—Satyrs, Browns, and Wood Nymphs

Subfamily **Elymniinae**

Tribe **Parargini**

Enodia portlandia (2,4)	**Pearly Eye H,K,O,OK,P,S**
	Pearly Wood Nymph
	Pearly Wood Butterfly
	Pearly-eyed Grayling

Southern Pearly Eye   So

p. floralae
p. missarkae
Enodia anthedon (1,2,3,4,C)   **Northern Pearly Eye**   M,O,OK,P,So,TS
Pearly Eye

Enodia creola (2,4)   **Creole Pearly Eye**   K,O,OK,P,So
Creole   H
Creola

Satyrodes eurydice (1,3,C)   **Eyed Brown**   K,M,O,OK,P,S,TS
Grass Nymph
Common Grass Nymph
Ten-spotted Quaker Butterfly
Eyed Grayling
Boisduval's Butterfly
Marsh-eyed Brown

e. fumosa   Smoky-eyed Brown   OK,P,TS
Satyrodes appalachia (1,2,3,4)   **Appalachian Eyed Brown**   M,O,OK
Appalachian Brown   P
Eyed Brown
Grass Nymph
Southern Eyed Brown
Woods Eyed Brown   So

a. leeuwi

Subfamily **Satyrinae—Satyrs and Wood Nymphs**

Tribe **Euptychiini—Wood Satyrs**

* Cyllopsis pyracmon (2)   **Pyracmon Brown**   TS
Mexican Arroyo Satyr   So

p. nabokovi   Nabokov's Satyr   P
Nabokov's Brown   TS

Cyllopsis henshawi (2)   **Henshaw's Brown**   H,TS
Sonoran Satyr   P
Henshaw's Quaker
Henshaw's Wood Nymph
Henshaw's Satyr

* Cyllopsis pertepida (1,2)   **Warm Brown**   TS
Arroyo Satyr   So

p. dorothea   Canyonland Satyr   P
Dorothy's Satyr

Nabokov's Wood Nymph
Grand Canyon Brown   TS
p. maniola   Arizona Brown   TS
p. avicula   Texas Brown
West Texas Brown   TS
Cyllopsis gemma (2,4)   **Gemmed Satyr**   K,O,OK,P
Gemmed Brown   H
Gem Quaker
Jeweled Satyr   So

g. freemani
* Hermeuptychia hermes (2,3,4)   **Hermes Satyr**   P
Southern Satyr   So
Hermeuptychia sosybius (4)   **Carolina Satyr**   K,O,OK,P
Carolina Brown
Carolinian Satyr   H
Dark Quaker
Neonympha areolata (2,3,4)   **Georgia Satyr**   K,O,OK,P,S
Georgian Satyr   H
Golden-ringed Quaker
Blue-spot Ringlet Butterfly
Orange-oval Satyr   So

a. septentrionalis
Neonympha mitchellii (3,4)   **Mitchell's Satyr**   H,K,O,OK
Mitchell's Marsh Satyr   P

m. sancticrucis
Megisto cymela (W)   **Little Wood Satyr**   H,K,M,O,OK,P,S,So
Eurytris Butterfly
Spotted Quaker Butterfly
Five-spotted Quaker
Dusky Argus
Six-spotted Quaker Butterfly
Wood Nymph
Megisto viola   Viola's Wood Satyr   O,OK
Megisto rubricata (2)   **Red Satyr**   H,K,O,P,So
Ruddy Quaker
r. smithorum   Smith's Red Satyr
r. cheneyorum   Arizona Red Satyr
Paramacera allyni (2)   **Pine Satyr**   P
Reakirt's Satyr   H

Allyn's Satyr
Mexican Pine Satyr So

Tribe **Coenonymphini—Ringlets**

Coenonympha haydenii (1)   **Hayden's Ringlet** P,TS
Wyoming Ringlet P
Hayden's Butterfly
Yellowstone Ringlet So

Coenonympha tullia (W)   **Ringlet** K,O,So
Large Heath P
Tullia Ringlet
Ochre Ringlet P
Small Ringlet M

t. kodiak   Kodiak Ringlet P,TS
Alaskan Ringlet H
Arctic Ringlet
Kodiak Quaker

t. yukonensis   Yukon Arctic Ringlet TS
Yukon Ringlet H

t. mixturata   Variable Arctic Ringlet
Arctic Ringlet TS

t. mcissaaci   McIsacc's Ringlet K

t. nipisquit   Nipisquit Ringlet P
Maritime Ringlet K

t. heinemani

t. inornata   Inornate Ringlet H,K,O,OK,TS
Prairie Ringlet P
Plain Yellow Quaker

t. benjamini   Prairie Ringlet H,K,TS
Plain Ringlet

t. mackenziei   Davenport's Ringlet TS

t. ochracea   Ochre Ringlet H,K,P,TS
Ochraceous Ringlet
Ochraceous Quaker

t. brenda   Utah Ringlet H
Great Basin Ringlet TS
Southern Yellow Quaker

t. subfusca   White Mountains Ringlet TS

t. furcae   Grand Canyon Ringlet H,TS

t. mono   Mono Ringlet TS

t. elko	Nevada Ringlet TS
	Elko Ringlet H
	Elko Yellow Quaker
t. columbiana	Columbian Ringlet H,TS
	Columbian Ochre Ringlet
t. eunomia	Dornfeld's Ringlet TS
	Dornfeld's Ochre Ringlet
t. ampelos	Northwest Ringlet P,TS
	Ringless Ringlet
	Ampelos Ringlet
	Ampelos Quaker
t. insulana	Vancouver Ringlet H
	Vancouver Island Ringlet TS
	Island Ochre Ringlet
t. california	California Ringlet H,P,TS
	Boisduval's Ringlet
	Californian Yellow Quaker
	White-dotted Quaker
t. eryngii	Siskiyou Ringlet TS
	Northern California Ringlet

Tribe **Maniolini**

Cercyonis pegala (W)	**Common Wood Nymph** M,O,OK
	Wood Nymph K,So,TS
	Large Wood Nymph P
	Blue-eyed Grayling P
	Grayling K
	Southern Wood Nymph H
	Goggle Eye So
	Southern Wood Butterfly
	Atlantic Grayling
p. abbotti	
p. alope	Blue-eyed Grayling S
	Blue-eyed Ringlet
	Smooth Hipparchy
	Alope Butterfly
	Brown Butterfly
	Yellow-spotted Wood Butterfly
	Yellow-spotted Butterfly
	Wood Nymph

	Blue-eyed Satyr
p. nephele	Dull-eyed Grayling S
	Clouded Wood Nymph H
	Brown Wood Butterfly
	Blind-eyed Grayling
	Clouded Hipparchia
	Cloudy Hipparchy
	Clouded Butterfly
	Blind-eyed Satyr
	Common Wood Nymph
p. olympus	Olympian Wood Nymph H,TS
p. texana	Texas Wood Nymph TS
p. ino	Hall's Wood Nymph TS
p. boopis	Ox-eyed Satyr TS
	Ox-eyed Wood Nymph H
	Boopis Satyr
	Baron's Satyr H
	Baron's Butterfly
	Hoary Satyr
p. ariane	Ariane Satyr H,TS
	Ariane's Butterfly
	Gabb's Butterfly
	Gabb's Satyr H
p. stephensi	Stephen's Satyr
	Light Satyr
p. wheeleri	Wheeler's Satyr H
	Wheeler's Butterfly
p. damei	Grand Canyon Satyr TS
Cercyonis meadii (1,2)	**Mead's Wood Nymph** P
	Mead's Satyr H,TS
	Red-eyed Nymph
	Red-eyed Wood Nymph P
	Mead's Butterfly
	Red Wood Nymph So
m. alamosa	Alamosa Satyr TS
m. melania	Wind's Satyr TS
m. mexicana	Chermock's Satyr TS
†*Cercyonis sthenele* (1,2,C)	**Great Basin Wood Nymph** P
	Least Wood Nymph H

	Behr's Satyr H
	Boisduval's Wood Nymph
	Scrub Wood Nymph So
	Woodland Satyr TS
	Sylvan Wood Nymph M
	Small Wood Nymph
	Sthenele Satyr
	San Francisco Butterfly
s. masoni	Mason's Satyr TS
	Mason's Wood Nymph
s. paulus	Little Satyr TS
	Small Wood Nymph H
	Paulus Butterfly
Cercyonis oetus (1,2,C)	**Dark Wood Nymph** M,P
	Least Satyr H,TS
	Small Wood Nymph So
	Least Wood Nymph
	California Wood Butterfly
o. charon	Charon Satyr TS
	Dark Wood Nymph H
	Charon Butterfly
o. silvestris	Sylvan Satyr H
	Sylvan Wood Nymph
	Sylvan Butterfly
	Little Satyr
	Phocus Satyr
	Woodland Satyr TS
o. pallescens	Pale Satyr TS

Tribe **Erebiini—Alpines**

Erebia vidleri (1,C)	**Vidler's Alpine** H,M,P,TS
	Northwest Alpine P
	Cascades Alpine So
Erebia rossii (A,C)	**Ross's Alpine** H,K,M,O,P,TS
	Arctic Alpine P
	Two-dot Alpine So
	Ross' Dusky Butterfly
r. ornata	Ornate Alpine TS
r. gabrieli	Gabriel's Alpine TS
r. kuskoquima	Kuskokwim Alpine TS

Erebia disa (1,A,C)   **Disa Alpine** K,M,O,OK,TS
                                  Spruce Bog Alpine P
                                  White-spot Alpine So
   d. mancinus   Mancinus Alpine H,TS
                                  North-western Dusky Butterfly
   d. steckeri   Stecker's Alpine H,TS
   d. subarctica   Subarctic Alpine TS
Erebia magdalena (1,2,A,C)   **Magdalena Alpine** M,P,TS
                                  Rockslide Alpine P,So
                                  Strecker's Alpine H
                                  Magdaleen's Butterfly
   m. mckinleyensis   Mt. McKinley Alpine TS
Erebia fasciata (A,C)   **Banded Alpine** H,M,O,P,TS
                                  White-banded Alpine
                                  Fasciated Butterfly
                                  White-band Alpine So
                                  Fasciata Alpine
   f. avinoffi   Avinoff's Alpine H,TS
   f. semo
Erebia discoidalis (W)   **Red-disked Alpine** H,K,M,O,OK,P,TS
                                  Red-streaked Alpine
                                  Red-disk Alpine So
                                  Discal Dusky Butterfly
   d. mcdunnoughi   McDunnough's Red-disked Alpine TS
Erebia theano (1,2,A,C)   **Theano Alpine** K,M,O,P,TS
                                  Banded Alpine So
   t. canadensis   Churchill Alpine TS
                                  Strecker's Dusky Butterfly
   t. alaskensis   Holland's Alpine
                                  Holland's Theano Alpine TS
   t. ethela   Ethel's Alpine TS
                                  Ethel's Butterfly
   t. demmia   Demmia Alpine TS
Erebia youngi (A,C)   **Young's Alpine** H,M,P,TS
                                  Yukon Alpine P
                                  Four-dot Alpine So
   y. herscheli   Herschel Island Alpine TS
   y. rileyi   Riley's Alpine TS
Erebia epipsodea (1,2,A,C)   **Common Alpine** H,K,M,O,P,So,TS

	Butler's Alpine P
	Dotted Dusky Butterfly
e. rhodia	Bruce's Alpine H
	Common Alpine TS
e. freemani	Freeman's Alpine TS
e. hopfingeri	Hopfinger's Alpine TS
e. remingtoni	Remington's Alpine TS
Erebia callias (1,2)	**Colorado Alpine** H,P
	Mead's Alpine TS
	Relict Gray Alpine So
	Colorado Dusky Butterfly
Erebia lafontainei (A,C)	**Reddish Four-dot Alpine** So
	Lafontaine's Alpine M
Erebia occulta (A,C)	**Eskimo Alpine** So
Erebia inuitica (A)	

Tribe **Pronophilini**

*Gyrocheilus patrobas (2)	**Red-bordered Brown** P
	Tritonia TS
	Red-rim Satyr So
p. tritonia	Arizona Blackamoor
	Triton Butterfly
	Tritonia H,TS

Tribe **Satyrini—True Satyrs**

Neominois ridingsii (1,2,C)	**Ridings' Satyr** H,M,O,TS
	Riding's Satyr P
	Grasshopper Satyr So
	Ridings' Butterfly
r. stretchii	Stretch's Satyr TS
	Dionysus Satyr
	Scudder's Satyr H
	Scudder's Wood Butterfly
r. pallidus	
r. minimus	
r. neomexicanus	
Oeneis nevadensis (1,2,C)	**Great Arctic** M,P,TS
	Nevada Arctic P
	Felder's Arctic H
	Pacific Arctic So

	Nevada Barren-ground Butterfly
	Californian Barren-ground Butterfly
	Nevada Grayling
n. gigas	Greater Arctic H
	Giant Arctic TS
	Giant Butterfly
	Great Grayling
n. iduna	Iduna Butterfly
	Iduna Arctic H,TS
Oeneis macounii (1,3,C)	**Macoun's Arctic** H,K,M,O,P,TS
	Canada Arctic P,So
Oeneis chryxus (W)	**Chryxus Arctic** H,K,M,O,P,TS
	Brown Arctic So
	Dull Orange Butterfly
c. calais	Chrysus Arctic OK
c. caryi	Cary's Arctic H,TS
c. valerata	Olympic Arctic TS
c. stanislaus	Hovanitz's Arctic TS
c. ivallda	California Arctic P
	Ivallda Arctic
	Mead's Arctic H
	Nevada Barren-ground Butterfly
Oeneis uhleri (1,2,A,C)	**Uhler's Arctic** H,M,O,OK,P,TS
	Rocky Mountain Arctic So
u. varuna	Varuna Arctic H,TS
	Uhler's Butterfly
u. nahanni	Dyar's Arctic H
	Nahanni Mountains Arctic TS
u. cairnesi	Cairnes' Arctic TS
u. reinthali	Reinthal's Arctic TS
Oeneis alberta (1,2,C)	**Alberta Arctic** M,O,P,TS
	Albertian Arctic H
	Prairie Arctic So
a. oslari	Oslar's Arctic TS
a. capulinensis	Capulin Arctic TS
a. daura	Daura Arctic
	Strecker's Arctic
Oeneis taygete (1,2,A,C)	**White-veined Arctic** K,O,P,TS
	Labrador Arctic H,P

	Taygete Butterfly
t. fordi	Ford's Arctic TS
t. edwardsi	Edwards' Arctic TS
t. gaspeensis	
Oeneis bore (1,2,A,C)	**Arctic Grayling** P,So
	Boreal Arctic TS
b. hanburyi	Boreal Arctic TS
b. mckinleyensis	Mt. McKinley Arctic TS
Oeneis jutta (W)	**Jutta Arctic K,M,O,OK,P,TS**
	Arctic Satyr S
	Nova Scotia Arctic H
	Barren-ground Butterfly
	Nova Scotian
	Nova Scotian Arctic
	Forest Arctic So
j. terraenovae	
j. ascerta	
j. ridingiana	Riding Mts. Arctic TS
	Jutta Arctic
j. harperi	
j. leussleri	Leussler's Jutta Arctic TS
j. alaskensis	Alaskan Jutta Arctic TS
j. chermocki	
j. reducta	Rocky Mountain Jutta Arctic TS
	Western Jutta Arctic
Oeneis melissa (1,2,3,A,C)	**Melissa Arctic** K,M,O,P,TS
	Mottled Arctic So
m. semidea	White Mountain Butterfly H,OK,P,S
	Norna Arctic
	White Mountain Arctic
	Mountain Butterfly
	Brown Mountain Butterfly
m. semplei	
m. assimilis	Mimicking Arctic H
	Butler's Arctic H
	Northern Melissa Arctic TS
m. gibsoni	Gibson's Melissa Arctic H,TS
m. beanii	Bean's Melissa Arctic H,TS
m. lucilla	Colorado Melissa Arctic TS

	Colorado Arctic
Oeneis polixenes (1,2,3,A,C)	**Polixenes Arctic** K,M,O,P,TS
	Fabrician Arctic H
	Crambis Butterfly
	Banded Arctic So
p. katahdin	Katahdin Arctic H,P
	Katahdin Butterfly
	Polixenes Arctic OK
p. subhyalina	Curtis' Arctic H
	Subhyaline Polixenes Arctic TS
	Arctic Barren Ground Butterfly
	Peart's Polixenes Arctic
p. yukonensis	Yukon Polixenes Arctic TS
p. brucei	Bruce's Arctic H
	Bruce's Polixenes Arctic TS
p. woodi	
Oeneis philipi (A,C)	
Oeneis excubitor (A,C)	**Sentinel Arctic** P,TS
	Eskimo Arctic So

Family DANAIDAE—Monarchs and Queens

Subfamily Danainae—Monarchs and Queens

Danaus plexippus (W)	**Monarch** H,Hw,K,M,O,OK,P,S,So,TS
	Milkweed Butterfly K
	Storm Fritillary
	Wanderer
	Archippus
Danaus gilippus (W)	**Queen** H,Hw,K,O,OK,P,So,TS
g. berenice	
g. strigosus	Striated Queen TS
Danaus eresimus (2,4)	**Soldier** O,So
	Tropic Queen
e. montezuma	Montezuma
e. tethys	Soldier OK

Subfamily Ituninae

*Lycorea cleobaea (2,4)	**Large Tiger** O,So

Tropical Milkweed Butterfly P
Fig Butterfly

c. demeter
c. atergatis   Ceres

Family **ITHOMIIDAE**

Dircenna klugii (2)   Klug's Dircenna H
* Greta polissena
p. umbrana

Bibliography

Abbot, J., and J. E. Smith. 1797. *The Natural History of the Rarer Lepidopterous Insects of Georgia*. T. Bensley, London. 200 pp.

Albrecht, C. W., and R. Watkins. 1983. *A Cross-Reference to Names of Ohio Skippers and Butterflies*. College of Biological Science, Ohio State University, Columbus, Ohio. 20 pp.

Barcant, M. 1970. *Butterflies of Trinidad and Tobago*. Collins, London. 314 pp.

Blackmore, E. H. 1927. *Checklist of the Macrolepidoptera of British Columbia*. British Columbia Provincial Museum, Victoria. 47 pp.

Brewer, J., and D. Winter. 1986. *Butterflies and Moths: A Companion to Your Field Guide*. Prentice Hall, New York. 224 pp.

Bridges, C. A. 1989. *Addenda/Corrigenda to the Supplement to: A Catalogue/Checklist of the Butterflies of America North of Mexico*. Privately published, Urbana, Illinois. 22 pp.

Brown, F. M., and B. Heineman. 1972. *Jamaica and Its Butterflies*. E. W. Classey, London. 484 pp.

Brown, F. M., J. D. Eff, and B. Rotger. 1957. *Colorado Butterflies*. Denver Museum of Natural History, Denver. 368 pp.

Christensen, J. R. 1981. *A Field Guide to the Butterflies of the Pacific Northwest*. Northwest Naturalist Books. University Press of Idaho, Moscow. 116 pp.

Clark, A. H. 1932. *The Butterflies of the District of Columbia and Vicinity*. U.S. Government Printing Office, Washington, D.C. 323 pp.

Comstock, J. A. 1927. *Butterflies of California*. Privately published, Los Angeles. 334 pp.

Comstock, J. H., and A. B. Comstock. 1929. *How to Know the Butterflies*. Comstock Publishing, Ithaca, New York. 311 pp.

Dornfeld, E. J. 1980. *The Butterflies of Oregon*. Timber Press, Forest Grove, Oregon. 276 pp.

Ebner, J. A. 1970. *Butterflies of Wisconsin*. Popular Science Handbook 12. Milwaukee Public Museum. 205 pp.

Ehrlich, P. R., and D. D. Murphy. 1982. Butterfly nomenclature: A critique. *Journal of Research on the Lepidoptera* 20(1): 1–11.

Ehrlich, P. R., and D. D. Murphy. 1983. Nomenclature, taxonomy, and evolution. *Journal of Research on the Lepidoptera* 20(4): 199–204.

Elrod, W. H. 1906. *The Butterflies of Montana*. Bulletin of the University of Montana 30: 1–174.

Emmel, T. C., and J. F. Emmel. 1973. *The Butterflies of Southern California*. Natural History Museum, Los Angeles. 140 pp.

Essig, E. O. 1926. *Insects of Western North America*. Macmillan, New York. 1035 pp.

Ferguson, D. C. 1955. *The Lepidoptera of Nova Scotia, Part I*. Nova Scotia Museum of Science, Halifax. 379 pp.

Ferris, C. D. (ed.). 1989. Supplement to: A catalogue/checklist of the butterflies of America north of Mexico. *Memoirs of the Lepidopterists' Society* 3: 1–103.

Ferris, C. D., and F. M. Brown. 1981. *Butterflies of the Rocky Mountain States.* University of Oklahoma Press, Norman. 442 pp.

Field, W. D. 1938 (1940). A manual of the butterflies and skippers of Kansas. *Bulletin of the University of Kansas* 39: 1–328.

Forbes, W. T. M. 1960. *The Lepidoptera of New York and Neighboring States, Part 4.* Entomological Reprint Specialists, East Lansing, Michigan. 188 pp.

Garth, J. S. 1950. Butterflies of Grand Canyon National Park. *Grand Canyon Natural History Association Bulletin* 11: 1–52.

Garth, J. S., and J. W. Tilden. 1987. *California Butterflies.* University of California Press, Berkeley and Los Angeles. xvi + 247 pp.

Gerberg, E. J., and R. H. Arnett, Jr. 1986. *Florida Butterflies.* Natural Science Publications, Baltimore, Maryland. v + 90 pp.

Gosse, P. H. 1840. *The Canadian Naturalist, a series of observations of the Natural History of Lower Canada.* Van Voorst, London. 372 pp.

Gunder, J. D. 1930. The butterflies of Los Angeles County, California. *Bulletin of the Southern California Academy of Sciences* 29(2): 1–59.

Harris, L., Jr. 1972. *The Butterflies of Georgia.* Revised edition. University of Oklahoma Press, Norman. 326 pp.

Heitzman, J., and J. E. Heitzman. 1987. *Butterflies and Moths of Missouri.* Missouri Department of Conservation, Jefferson City. vii + 385 pp.

Holland, W. J. 1915. *The Butterfly Guide.* Doubleday, Garden City, New York. 237 pp.

Holland, W. J. 1931. *The Butterfly Book.* Revised edition. Doubleday, Garden City, New York. 424 pp.

Hooper, R. H. 1973. *The Butterflies of Saskatchewan.* Saskatchewan Department of Resources, Regina. 216 pp.

Howe, W. H. (ed.). 1975. *The Butterflies of North America.* Doubleday, New York. 637 pp.

Huth, E. J. 1978. *Council of Biology Editors Style Manual.* Council of Biology Editors, Arlington, Virginia. xvii + 265 pp.

Irwin, R. R., and J. C. Downey. 1973. Annotated checklist of the butterflies of Illinois. *Illinois Natural History Survey, Biological Notes* 81: 1–60.

Jenkins, D. W. 1984. *Hamadryas* in the United States (Nymphalidae). *Journal of the Lepidopterists' Society* 38(3): 171–175.

Johnson, K., and E. L. Quinter. 1983. Commentary on Miller and Brown versus Ehrlich and Murphy et al.: Pluralism in systematics and the worldwide nature of kinship groups. *Journal of Research on the Lepidoptera* 21(4): 255–269.

Jones, J. R. J. L. 1951. An annotated checklist of the Macrolepidoptera of British Columbia. *Entomological Society of British Columbia Occasional Papers* 1: 1–148.

Kimball, C. P. 1965. *The Lepidoptera of Florida.* Division of Plant Industry, Florida Deptartment of Agriculture, Gainesville. 363 pp.

Klots, A. B. 1951. *A Field Guide to the Butterflies East of the Great Plains.* Houghton Mifflin, Boston. 349 pp.

Lambremont, E. N. 1954. Butterflies and skippers of Louisiana. *Tulane Studies in Zoology* 10: 125–164.

Leighton, B. V. 1946. The butterflies of Washington. *University of Washington Publications in Biology* 9(2): 47–53.

Lenczewski, B. 1980. *Butterflies of Everglades National Park.* National Park Service, Homestead, Florida. 110 pp.

Linnaeus, C. [C. von Linné] 1758. *Systema Naturae per Regna Tria Naturae.* 10th edition. Holmiae, Uppsala. 824 pp.

Luquet, G. C. 1986. Les noms vernaculaires français des Rhopalocères d'Europe (Lepidoptera Rhopalocera). *Alexanor* 14(7) (Suppl.): 1–49.

Macy, R. W., and H. H. Shepard. 1941. *Butterflies: A Handbook of the Butterflies.* University of Minnesota Press, Minneapolis. 247 pp.

Mather, B. 1983. Critique of the *Audubon Field Guide. Southern Lepidopterists' News* 5: 3.

Maynard, C. J. 1881. *A Manual of North American Butterflies.* DeWolfe, Fiske, Boston. 226 pp.

Metcalf, C. L., and W. P. Flint. 1939. *Destructive and Useful Insects.* McGraw-Hill, New York. 1071 pp.

Miller, L. D. 1991. *A Field Guide to the Butterflies of Canada and Alaska.* Domino, London.

Miller, L. D., and F. M. Brown. 1981. A catalogue/checklist of the butterflies of America north of Mexico. *Memoirs of the Lepidopterists' Society* 2: 1–280.

Miller, L. D., and F. M. Brown. 1983. Butterfly taxonomy: A reply. *Journal of Research on the Lepidoptera* 20(4): 193–198.

Mitchell, R. T., and H. S. Zim. 1964. *Butterflies and Moths: A Guide to the More Common American Species.* Golden Press, New York. 160 pp.

Moore, S. 1960. A revised annotated list of the butterflies of Michigan. *Journal of the Lepidopterists' Society* 27: 302–303.

Morris, R. F. 1980. *Butterflies and Moths of Newfoundland and Labrador.* Agriculture Canada Publication 1691. 407 pp.

Murphy, D. D., and P. R. Ehrlich. 1983. Crows, bobs, tits, elfs, and pixies: The phoney "common name" phenomenon. *Journal of Research on the Lepidoptera* 22(2): 154–158.

Murphy, D. D., and P. R. Ehrlich. 1984. On butterfly taxonomy. *Journal of Research on the Lepidoptera* 23(1): 19–34.

Nabokov, V. 1945. Notes on neotropical Plebejinae. *Psyche* 52: 1–61.

Neill, W. A., and D. J. Hepburn. 1976. *Butterflies Afield in the Pacific Northwest.* Pacific Search Books, Seattle. 95 pp.

Opler, P. A. 1992. *Butterflies of Eastern North America and Greenland.* Houghton Mifflin, Boston.

Opler, P. A., and G. O. Krizek. 1984. *Butterflies East of the Great Plains.* Johns Hopkins University Press, Baltimore. 294 pp.

Orsak, L. J. 1977. *Butterflies of Orange County, California.* University of California Press, Irvine. 349 pp.

Parkes, K. C. 1978. A guide to forming and capitalizing compound names of birds in English. *Auk* 95: 324–326.

Powell, J. A., and C. L. Hogue. 1979. *California Insects.* University of California Press, Berkeley and Los Angeles. 388 pp.

Pyle, R. M. 1974. *Watching Washington Butterflies.* Trailside Series. Seattle Audubon Society. 109 pp.

Pyle, R. M. 1981. *The Audubon Society Field Guide to North American Butterflies.* Alfred A. Knopf, New York. 916 pp.

Pyle, R. M. 1984a. *The Audubon Society Handbook for Butterfly Watchers*. Scribner's, New York. 274 pp.

Pyle, R. M. 1984b. Rebuttal to Murphy and Ehrlich on common names of butterflies. *Journal of Research on the Lepidoptera* 23(1): 89–93.

Pyle, R. M. 1989. *Washington Butterfly Status Report and Conservation Plan*. Washington Department of Wildlife, Nongame Program, Olympia. 3 pp.

Riley, N. D. 1975. *Field Guide to the Butterflies of The West Indies*. Collins, London. 224 pp.

Saunders, A. A. 1932. *Butterflies of Allegany State Park*. University of the State of New York, Albany. 270 pp.

Scott, J. A. 1986. *The Butterflies of North America*. Stanford University Press, Stanford, California. 583 pp.

Scudder, S. H. 1877. English names for butterflies. *Psyche* 1: 2–3, 10–11, 31, 40, 43–44, 56.

Scudder, S. H. 1889. *The Butterflies of the Eastern United States and Canada with Special Reference to New England*. Privately published, Cambridge, Massachusetts. Three vols., 1958 pp.

Scudder, S. H. 1893. *Brief Guide to the Commoner Butterflies of the Northern United States and Canada*. Henry Holt, New York. 206 pp.

Scudder, S. H. 1895. *Frail Children of the Air*. Privately published, Boston. 186 pp.

Shapiro, A. M. 1966. *Butterflies of the Delaware Valley*. Special publication. American Entomological Society, Philadelphia. 79 pp.

Shapiro, A. M. 1974. Butterflies and skippers of New York State. *Search* 4: 1–60.

Shapiro, A. M. 1975. Review of *Watching Washington Butterflies*. *Journal of the Lepidopterists' Society* 29(2): 74–75.

Shull, E. M. 1987. *Indiana Butterflies*. Indiana Academy of Science/Indiana University Press, Bloomington. viii + 262 pp.

Sperling, F. A. H. 1987. Evolution of the *Papilio machaon* species group in Western Canada (Lepidoptera: Papilionidae). *Quaestiones Entomologicae* 23: 198–315.

Steinhauser, S. R. 1989. Taxonomic notes and descriptions of new taxa in the neotropical Hesperiidae. Part I. Pyrginae. *Bulletin of the Allyn Museum* 127: 1–70.

Stiling, P. D. 1989. *Florida's Butterflies and Other Insects*. Pineapple Press, Sarasota, Florida. 95 pp.

Stoetzel, M. B. 1989. *Common Names of Insects & Related Organisms 1989*. Entomological Society of America, College Park, Maryland. 197 pp.

Tietz, H. M. 1952. *The Lepidoptera of Pennsylvania: A Manual*. Pennsylvania Agricultural Experimental Station/Pennsylvania State College School of Agriculture, University Park. 194 pp.

Tilden, J. W. 1965. *Butterflies of the San Francisco Bay Region*. University of California Press, Berkeley and Los Angeles. 88 pp.

Tilden, J. W. and A. C. Smith. 1986. *A Field Guide to Western Butterflies*. Houghton Mifflin, Boston. 370 pp.

Tyler, H. A. 1975. *The Swallowtail Butterflies of North America*. Naturegraph, Healdsburg, California. 192 pp.

Underhill, J. E., and A. Harcombe. 1970. Moths and butterflies of Manning Park, British Columbia. *Parks Branch* 1: 1–9.

Index

119